D0483958

THE UNIVERSE IS CALLING YOU

ALSO BY CHAR MARGOLIS

Questions from Earth, Answers from Heaven

Discover Your Inner Wisdom

Love Karma

Life: A Spiritual Intuitive's Collection of Inspirational Thoughts

THE UNIVERSE IS CALLING YOU

Connecting with Essence to Live with Positive Energy, Love, and Power

CHAR MARGOLIS

WITH VICTORIA ST. GEORGE

ST. MARTIN'S
ESSENTIALS
NEW YORK

First published in the United States by St. Martin's Essentials,
an imprint of St. Martin's Publishing Group

www.stmartins.com

Book design by Richard Oriolo

The Library of Congress Cataloging-in-Publication Data

Names: Margolis, Char, author. | St. George, Victoria, author.
Title: The universe is calling you: connecting with essence to live with positive energy, love, and power / Char Margolis with Victoria St. George.
Description: First Edition. | New York: St. Martin's Essentials, 2020.
Identifiers: LCCN 2019037548 | ISBN 9781250258694 (hardcover) | ISBN 9781250258700 (ebook)
Subjects: LCSH: Self-actualization (Psychology) | Conduct of life—Miscellanea. | Love.
Classification: LCC BF637.S4 M3517 2020 | DDC 155.2—dc23
LC record available at https://lccn.loc.gov/2019037548

Our books may be purchased in bulk for promotional, educational, or business use.
Please contact your local bookseller or the Macmillan Corporate and
Premium Sales Department at 1-800-221-7945, extension 5442,
or by email at MacmillanSpecialMarkets@macmillan.com.

First Edition: February 2020

10 9 8 7 6 5 4 3 2 1

This book is dedicated to
the Essence in all of us.

CONTENTS

FOREWORD

When my mother was pregnant with me, a psychic told her, "You're gonna have a boy, and he'll be very famous." I lived my life believing that, and believing that there are other levels of consciousness available to us all. I came to realize we are all extensions of the power that created the whole universe. I first met Char Margolis in the mid-nineties, when Michelle Visage and I cohosted a morning-drive radio show at WKTU in NYC. Char would do live readings for callers and we kept bringing her back because she was helping so many people. It was during one of her visits to the show that she told me I would be well known on television, unbeknownst to her, validating what the psychic had told my mother many years before. I was just beginning my VH1 show.

I was always interested in the psychic energetic world and intuition. I had been aware of it my whole life. There is so much psychic debris in our world, and my goal has always been to resonate with the positive energy. I've been through many ups and downs, and I've learned that the dark clouds will pass. Darkness cannot exist in the presence of light. On my journey I've found those whom I resonate with who are beacons of light and seekers of wisdom. I believe we resonate with like kind. There are those of us who are part of "our tribe" and our goal is to clear the path for healing. Char is one of our tribe. All of us support one another because the waters can get very murky.

When you become the image of your own imagination and live with your truth, it's the most powerful thing you can ever do. I have practiced manifesting my destiny. This book brilliantly talks about manifestation and how you can apply it to your life. I grew up reading books like *The Universe Is Calling You* and I have always been a seeker. It's not only important to hear the call, but to recognize the voice. I listened to that guidance at pivotal moments and it was life changing for me. I listened because I had faith. If you hang in there long enough you will make a breakthrough. The Universe is calling you so we all need to be brave enough to answer. We don't need to make apologies for seeking higher knowledge. Sometimes we may make mistakes but that is how we learn. Char's book is filled with answers that will guide you to finding peace and happiness. It will help you decipher between positive and negative energies and keep you on the path of positive healing. All of us have a purpose in life. This guide can help you find your soul's purpose. First, understand if you can't love yourself how in the hell are you gonna love somebody else. As Char writes in this book, the first true love is self-love. It doesn't mean you're selfish, it means your needs matter. Give yourself the gift of wisdom and allow this book to help you find your essence and the core of who you really are. Be open enough to hear the call! Everybody say love! This book is filled with it! The Universe is calling you, LOVE, so listen!

—RuPaul

No matter what changes in each of our reincarnated lifetimes, our energy pattern stays with us. We all have our own energy thumbprint that identifies us through eternity. Our goal is to become one with goodness, love and God. Which is our Essence.

—Char Margolis

THE UNIVERSE IS CALLING YOU

ONE

Discovering Your True Self

"Who am I?"

"Why was I born?"

"What's my reason for living?"

"Why do the people I love have to die, and will I see them again?"

"Why do *I* have to die, and what will happen when I do?"

"Is this world all there is, or is there something more?"

"Why is there so much sorrow and evil in the world?"

"Is God really there?"

As a psychic intuitive medium for more than forty-five years, I have heard questions like these from thousands of people—clients, friends, family members, audiences of my TV shows, the people who attend book signings or whom I meet on the street. And I have asked these questions myself, especially in times of grief and emotional distress. I, too, have felt the enormous pain of losing loved ones, and the guilt and remorse and regret for things done and not done. And, like most people, there have been times that I have questioned the wisdom of a God that would allow famine, genocide, and suffering in the world.

However, the one thing I do *not* question—indeed, the thing I know with absolute certainty—is that we continue to live beyond the short time we spend on Earth in any given lifetime. Our souls exist before we are born, and our spirits do not die when our bodies stop working. I know this because my life's work is to connect people on Earth with the spirits of their departed loved ones. It is enormously rewarding. I have watched joy and amazement appear on the faces of fathers, mothers, sons, daughters, brothers, sisters, grandchildren, spouses, or best friends as they hear messages, through me, that could only come from the people who have passed over to the other side. I have witnessed the healing and consolation they feel when they know their loved ones are still there, still caring, still communicating and still connected to them despite the great loss from their death.

I saw this happen on one of my Dutch television shows. Thom's wife, Mariska, had died two years earlier, and he was still heartbroken. I went to his apartment in Amsterdam to give him a reading. Now, when I read for people, I usually pick up on the letters of the names of their loved ones, both living and deceased; it's my way of tuning in to the unique energy each spirit possesses. Within a minute or two, I picked up on the name of Thom's father, who was living, and then Maria, his wife's mother. "Maria is with Mariska and helping her to come through," I said. "Now Mariska is showing me something around your neck. What is it?"

Thom pulled out a pendant from under his shirt. "It contains her ashes," he told me.

"She knows that you wear it. She's also telling me about a colleague of yours that plays music. Are you a musician too?"

Thom sighed. "I was—but I stopped after she died." It was clear he was still in a great deal of pain.

"I know that a part of you stopped living when she died, but it makes her sad to think that you're not playing music," I told him. "She says that you're brilliant and gifted and talented and if you were to start being creative again, it would bring her closer to you. She says that there's music you need to write."

"I wrote something and performed it, but not recently," Thom admitted.

"Now she's showing me something about the heart." I tapped the upper part of my chest. "Did you two have a sign about the heart?"

Thom thought a moment, then he nodded. "I had a special tattoo done for her; it's her family initials. How could you know that?" And he pulled at his shirt to show me the tattoo in the same location where I had tapped my own chest.

But Mariska wasn't done. "When you cremated her, you put something on her heart or in her pocket? And nobody knows about it but you?" I asked.

Thom looked amazed. "I put a photo in with her, right above her heart. I did that at the cremation place; nobody saw me."

"She's saying, 'If you want proof that I'm still with you, your picture is on my heart and nobody knows it.'" Then I smiled and told Thom, "And she's saying that if you don't get your butt in gear and start writing music, she's going to be very mad!"

The connection we feel with our loved ones is one of the strongest forces in the universe. For most of us, it is a fundamental part of our lives, and well it should be—because love never dies. This reading brought Thom a great comfort because he knew that his beloved wife was still with him, still connected to him and watching over him, and she would be waiting for him when it was his time to pass over. It also provided him a cosmic kick to help him reconnect to life and make the most of his time here on Earth.

**Only with the heart can a person see rightly;
what is essential is invisible to the eye.**

—ANTOINE DE SAINT-EXUPÉRY

I believe that part of my mission on Earth is to give people proof that even after death their loved ones are still with them, so they can know that this life is *not* all there is, and that we all will continue to live and love for eternity. For more than forty-five years, I have been teaching my students, "Life is a school," "Cherish your loved ones every day," "Live in such a way that you will have no regrets," "You are part of something far greater than yourself," and "You can tap into the universal energy of goodness, wisdom, and love and use its guidance to prevent problems and guide your life." However, the core of my work goes beyond connecting people with departed loved ones, or even proving that there is life after death. The central part of my mission is to teach people how to develop their own intuition, their own inner wisdom, the innate sense inside of each one of us that is connected to everything, including the spirits of our departed loved ones. But equally important, my goal is to help people become aware of the universal wisdom, goodness, and love that unite everyone and everything. That universal goodness is where we come from when we are born, and where we return when we pass over to the other side.

Before You Were Born, You Lived

We are luminous beings. We are perceivers.
We are an awareness.

—DON JUAN, SHAMAN

We all start life as part of something other than ourselves. Our physical bodies are made from the genetic material of our parents; we are part of our mother biologically for nine months until we are separated physically at birth. But where does our animating spirit come from? When do we become the separate *I* consciousness of Char, or Thom, or Mariska, or you? And if that *I* consciousness is who we are during our lifetime, what happens to it when the physical body dies? These are questions that scientists and philosophers have wrestled with for centuries, and I'm not going to pretend that I know the answers. Indeed, any answer created by an incarnate human being is inevitably born of our human (and limited) experience and understanding. But I do know that there is a greater truth than any one of us can put into words, a truth that each of us knows intuitively and innately: *We are part of something far bigger than ourselves.* We are all on an eternal journey, and each individual lifetime is only a temporary stage in our progress. Before we were born, we lived. After we die, our spirits continue to learn and grow. Who we are when we are born, who we choose as our family (yes, we choose our parents and our family situation), and what we do with our lives are all part of something greater than our own individual experience in one particular lifetime.

I believe that each of us has always existed and will always continue to exist, because we are part of God. God was, is, and always will be; but divine energy is dynamic, not static. It creates the universe from itself, watches as it grows and expands and then disappears, to reappear in a new form. God is ever evolving, ever changing, yet always present. As part of this divine energy, we, too, grow and evolve. I believe that each of us starts off at the right hand of God, and we incarnate so we can learn lessons and grow from our experiences on Earth. As many spiritual masters tell us, we are pure Beings that become human for a while. During those incarnations we have free will and choice. We go through temptations and tests; we may take actions that can turn us to evil and others that turn us to good. In every incarnation, our goal is to learn and grow so much that we may get back to where we began—at the right hand of God, the ultimate in goodness and love, and whose goodness and love is expanded by our efforts. This eternal cycle of growth is our purpose and our nature, because it is the nature of the divine to continually evolve into ever-greater perfection.

In the realm of eternity, each of us has a *soul,* an energetic being that records and benefits from the lessons and experiences of all our times on Earth. The soul's reason for existence is to learn and grow in goodness, wisdom, and love. But while souls make progress in the eternal realm, the greatest progress happens here on Earth. That's why we are born and live many lives; Earth is our school, and here is where we learn our most important lessons. When our soul chooses to come to Earth and be born, we become what I call a *spirit.* Each spirit has a unique energy thumbprint, based upon its experiences in each lifetime. That unique energy is what we sense when someone we love walks into a room and, without seeing or hearing them, we know who it is. We keep our energy thumbprint even after we die; in fact, that is what I pick up on when I sense the presence of a departed loved one on the other side. At the same time, part of us stays with the soul in the spirit world even while we incarnate here on Earth. I think of it kind of like dreaming. When we dream, part of us is in the dream and fully experiencing it. For the part of us in the dream, it seems "real." Yet at the same time there also is part of us lying on a bed, sleeping, seemingly unconscious of our surroundings unless something wakes us up. Two parts of the same being, two parts of our consciousness, coexisting in the same moment, connected yet unaware of the connection—that's how I view the eternal connection between the incarnated spirit and the eternal soul.

We are born as many different spirits in many different forms—men, women, beasts, of all shapes, sizes, colors, and abilities. In these forms, we are confronted with all the lessons life has to give us: love, betrayal, temptation, guilt, making right choices, and so on. In each lifetime, we also have glimpses that remind us that we are not bodies with spirits but spirits with bodies. When the body dies, the spirit returns to its eternal form as intelligent energy. Think of your spirit as a snowflake. Each snowflake is unique, formed by water vapor in the atmosphere that freezes and takes solid form. The snowflake falls to Earth, where it melts and turns back into water. Eventually the water evaporates, rises to the clouds, and the cycle begins again. Like that snowflake, your soul takes a unique and beautiful spirit form so it might come to Earth. When you die, your spirit returns to its original state and rejoins the soul on the other side. But that doesn't mean our spirits lose their unique energy or stop being connected to our loved ones.

Even after death, each spirit continues to care about friends and family here on Earth and those who have already passed over. Love never dies, and our spirits are part of an immense web of love that crosses the barrier of death and continues from lifetime to lifetime. That web of love and connection is why we can sense the presence of our loved ones after they are gone. It's why people who are dying often see their loved ones waiting for them with open arms. The ongoing connection is the reason we have soul mates, people whom we love lifetime after lifetime. That web of love enables me (and you) to tune in to the spirits on the other side and give their messages to their loved ones on Earth.

When we pass over, in the moment of our death, our life flashes before our eyes. We see our thoughts and deeds through the eyes of truth and goodness. (In life, people may go into denial, but in the afterlife, we cannot ignore the truth.) We see what we have learned as well as the lessons we have failed to learn. Our spirit then rejoins our soul, which adds the experiences from this lifetime to the memories of all the past lifetimes we have gone through over the ages. Each lifetime is an opportunity either to move higher or to create karma that must be cleared before the soul can progress. If we learn our lessons well and we grow in goodness, wisdom, and love, our soul becomes more and more refined; it vibrates at a higher level. Souls that vibrate at higher levels may become guardian angels, or they may choose to come back as great beings that inspire us with their examples. If our soul has not learned all its lessons or has more growing to do, it goes back to "school"—Earth—and reincarnates as a spirit again. If while on Earth a spirit chooses to cause deliberate harm or to do evil in some way, that energy, too, is added to our soul, which then vibrates at a lower level and *must* reincarnate to make amends in some way. It's called the law of karma: what you sow in one lifetime, you will reap in the next. Only when the past karma of evil deeds is atoned for can your soul continue its progress.

> The soul is timeless. A spiritual part of all creation, it is formed from the loving energy that creates us all.
>
> —HOWARD F. BATIE

If the goal of the spirit is to learn and grow in each lifetime, and if the goal of the soul is to incorporate the wisdom of each spirit's experience and use it to grow in goodness, wisdom, and love, what happens when the soul is completely filled with these energies? I believe that the ultimate destination of our soul's progress is the truth of who we truly are. *We are manifestations of the intelligent, loving energy that composes the universe.* We are all part of that universal consciousness, an interconnected energy that creates reality in every moment. This energy contains good and bad, great and small, the universe itself and every manifestation present within it. It existed before time and will exist after time ends. This energy goes by many names: *qi* or *chi* (Chinese), *prana* (Indian), *mana* (Polynesian), *ni* (Native American), *num* (African), *vital fluid, the field of infinite possibilities, quantum soup, the life force, morphic energy,* and so on. But it is universal *conscious* energy: it is both intelligent and beneficent. It is both what we are made of and also a force that wants the best for us. Religious leaders and philosophers have personalized this energy, calling it *God, Yahweh, Being, the Tao, Atman, Allah, Universal Consciousness, Light, the Divine, Oneness, the Over-soul,* and a thousand other terms that cannot begin to describe it. I have come to call this universal, loving goodness *Essence,* because it is the force that lies at the core of every being, every experience, every leaf, star, atom, and galaxy. It is also the essential truth of who we are.

Essence Is Essential

Something there is in every drop of water, every grain of sand, which it is beyond the power of human understanding to fathom or comprehend.

—GEORGE BERKELEY, IRISH BISHOP AND PHILOSOPHER

The root of the word *essence* comes from the Latin word *esse,* which means "to be." The definition of *essence* is "the basic, real, and invariable nature of a thing or its significant individual feature or features: the most important part or quality." Philosophy says that *essence* is "the inward nature, true substance, or constitution of anything, as opposed to what is accidental, phenomenal, illusory, etc." Essence is essential; it is the component that makes something what it is, and without which that "thing" would be different.

I use the term *Essence* to describe the *fundamental, living, intelligent, loving energy that makes up the entire universe and everything beyond it.* The same love, the same divine energy, the same wisdom that can power the atoms and speak to us from beyond the grave is who we truly are. No name can capture it because this energy transcends any words or concepts that can be created by our limited human minds. For centuries, poets and philosophers of every great religious and spiritual tradition have tried to describe this living and intelligent Essence. In Psalm 111, David says the Lord is "honorable," "glorious," "righteous," "gracious," and "full of compassion." John 1:9 describes *Essence* as "the light that gives light to every man." The Bhagavad Gita says *Essence* is "the taste of water, the light of the sun and moon, the sound in ether and ability in man; . . . the original fragrance of the earth, the heat in fire, the intelligence of the intelligent and the strength of the strong," an energy in everything and yet independent. The *Tao Te Ching* describes the Tao as "the Mother of all things." Zen Buddhists call Essence the state of Absolute Being—undivided, eternal, and holy. On the very first page of the Koran, Allah, which literally means "the divine," is said to be benevolent and merciful; Allah creates and maintains all things and brings them to a state of perfection.

Both your soul and spirit are made of this essential energy. You are simply a part of Essence that has chosen to become a human being in this point of space-time. Remember the snowflake, beautiful and unique, forming in a cloud, drifting to Earth, then becoming water, then vapor, and ascending once more to the clouds? The snowflake's essence is always the same—water. Each time we incarnate as human beings, we take form and come to Earth for a certain amount of time, to live and love and learn our lessons. After a while, our physical form disappears and we transform back into our original, essential energy. No matter what form we take, our Essence remains the same.

> At the heart of each of us, whatever our imperfections,
> there exists a silent pulse of perfect rhythm, which is
> absolutely individual and unique, and yet
> which connects us to everything else.
>
> —GEORGE LEONARD

Our Essence is always there even when we're not aware of it, because it's all around us. We're like the little fish that spent its entire life happily swimming in a cove next to a beach. Then one day it heard one of the other fish speaking of something it called the "ocean." "It's the biggest thing you've ever seen," the other fish said. "You can't imagine how huge and wonderful it is." The little fish was fascinated. Nothing would do but it had to go in search of the ocean. It swam out of its cove and far out into the ocean waters, where it encountered a wise old fish.

"Excuse me, but can you tell me how to find the ocean?" the little fish asked.

"You're in it right now—it's all around you," the other fish replied.

"But this is just water," the little fish said, disappointed. "I'm looking for the ocean, which is the biggest thing anyone could imagine." And it swam off in an endless search for the place where it already was.

Some spiritual masters and traditions tell us that we must seek long and hard, meditate for hours, fast for days, or give up our material possessions to discover our Essence. I'm here to tell you, however, that you *have* experienced Essence. In fact, you're experiencing it in every moment—you simply may never have used the term *Essence* to describe it. Like the little fish, you are swimming in the ocean of Essence, but you aren't aware of exactly where you are. But connecting to Essence can be as simple as closing your eyes and focusing on its presence within.

CONNECTING TO ESSENCE

Close your eyes for a moment and focus on your breath as it comes in and out. You don't have to do anything to earn the right to breathe—it's natural. As you focus on your breath, notice the subtle energy in your body. There's a sense of aliveness that includes your conscious mind yet is bigger than just your thoughts or your body. That subtle energy is Essence. If you don't feel it, relax. It's always there, and it never changes, because it's who you really are. Eventually, your mind will allow you to feel your Essence.

Connecting to Essence can happen when we listen to the voice inside us that tells us what choice will be our highest and best. It can happen when we walk out of our front door and appreciate the miracles of nature. It can happen when we see the smile of a baby, hear the voice of a loved one, or feel the hug of a friend. We connect with Essence anytime we recognize that we are not alone, that we are part of something greater than ourselves, and who we are will survive the death of the physical body as our spirits step gently from this world into the next. When we connect with Essence, we remember that, while there is good and evil in this world, we are here to choose the good. Every time we choose good over evil, we strengthen the presence of Essence in our lives. When we feel it, our lives are happier and more complete.

In moments when our emotions are heightened, it can feel as if we move toward a greater awareness of Essence. When a mother holds her child in her arms for the first time. When family and loved ones gather for a dying person's last moments. When we look into the eyes of our soul mate. In times of great tragedy, like the terrorist attacks in New York, Washington, London, Madrid, or Bali, we can feel Essence upholding and strengthening us. In times of celebration, we can sense a happiness that is beyond the personal and connects us to something deeper. There are moments in life where we rely on God's will, and we can feel truth and pureness radiating from within and outside of ourselves. In all of these experiences, Essence shines forth, if we are simply willing to acknowledge its presence. Rabbi Irwin Kula says that at these times, the only way to describe our emotions is with the expression "Oh my God!"—an instant recognition of the presence of Essence. With each instance, our perception of Essence is clearer, and we will feel its love and support in our lives in every possible circumstance. Essence is joy, bliss, connectedness to everything. Essence is like the air you breathe—always present, rarely noticed, but essential for life.

Letting Your True Nature Shine Forth

In the same way that we can keep an intimate relationship fresh and alive by focusing on the love we share with a partner, acknowledging the gift our partner is in our life, and appreciating the little ways our partner makes us feel loved, we can nurture our relationship with Essence by paying attention to it, by focusing on the gifts it brings to us, and by looking for the ways that it appears in every minute. However, when we are faced with tragic loss that we can't understand, we can feel cut off from Essence. I once read for a young mother who had gone through one of the most difficult experiences any parent could face: she had accidentally left her baby son, Chris, in the back seat of the family car. It was a hot day, and the little boy died before she returned. When I visited her several months later, it was clear that she was still heartbroken, racked with guilt and remorse. As compassionately as I could, I told her, "You can't put yourself through this torture. This was an accident, completely unintentional, and your son knows that. His spirit is around you, and if he sees mama sad all the time, he won't understand it. He's so little that he didn't know he passed over—he's just playing in heaven, and he's with your family on the other side."

For a moment the mother looked as if she felt better, but then she started to cry. "Why didn't someone see him?" she asked in despair. "No one stopped, no one looked in the car the entire time I was gone, no one called me from day care to ask where he was. Why didn't my intuition warn me? Why wasn't a guardian angel watching over my little boy?" Her husband took her hand and tried to console her, but it was clear that his heart was close to breaking, too.

"Maybe a guardian angel *was* watching over him," I answered, trying not to cry myself. "Maybe God needed Chris more than you did, and his guardian angel took him straight to heaven. Sometimes children who go to heaven young are here to share their love with us for a short time and then move on. This was just a really sad mistake, but you need to forgive yourself." The mom looked doubtful, but her baby's spirit was speaking clearly through me. "Chris is still with you," I reassured her. "He's happy and loving and being taken care of on the other side. And I hope you will come to feel the peace he's letting me feel right now." Something of Chris's spirit must have been speaking silently to his parents, because I could see their energy getting lighter.

My work of connecting people like these grieving parents with their departed loved ones can bring consolation and closure. It also can give people in pain the confidence that those they love and have lost are still alive and happy. But ultimately the highest goal of a reading is to open people's hearts and minds to the Essence of goodness, wisdom, and love of which we are made and in which we exist. How much better would you feel knowing that even in the most tragic circumstances there was a conscious energy of goodness, wisdom, and love that was looking out for you and for those you love? Better yet, how would it be to be able to connect to that very same energy at any moment in time? Living in Essence shows us how to deal with fear, with crisis, with catastrophe. When we are connected with our inner truth and divinity, we can face our fears and either overcome them or use them as the warnings they are. And while living in Essence does not mean we are immune to the challenges of life, it does give us a rock upon which to stand as the waves of crisis and catastrophe wash against us. As Psalm 23 says, "Though I walk through the valley of the shadow of death, I will fear no evil, for you are with me."

When we live in Essence, we know that universal wisdom is always with us, present inside our hearts and minds. The more we acknowledge it and seek to connect with it, the more it can manifest for us every day. Sometimes your Essence will be like the sun breaking through the clouds, sometimes it will completely take over the sky, and sometimes it will rest behind the horizon. But remember, your Essence is the most constant part of you, or me, or us, and your spirit and soul.

Intuition and Essence

Intuition is one of the primary ways we can connect directly with Essence. Do you ever have moments when your intuition pops up and you know without a doubt that this is the answer? In the same way, when we get a glimpse of Essence, that same familiarity touches our entire being and reminds us of our true purpose for existence. Intuition is our direct pipeline to the all-knowing nature of Essence, and when we use it to tune in, we also can sense the loving side of Essence as well. And the more we use our intuition or connect with Essence, the stronger and easier it becomes to hear its message.

However, if you're trying too hard to connect, you can get in your own way. If you've ever "tried" to meditate, you know what I mean. Sitting down and thinking, *I want to meditate . . . I want to meditate . . . Why am I still thinking? I want to meditate!* is the surest recipe for failure and frustration. In the same way, working too hard to be intuitive or to be aware of Essence causes you to focus on the effort rather than the goal. You don't have to work to be intuitive, and you don't have to work to be aware of Essence, any more than you have to work hard to *be.* I tell my students who are studying to develop their intuition, "If you have to work hard at this, you're doing it wrong. Know you are intuitive, do what you need to do to clear your mind and calm your body and emotions; then ask your question, let go, and trust. Often your intuition will give you the answer when you least expect it." The same is true of connecting with Essence. Clear your mind, calm your body, and then turn your focus inside. Listen for the subtle energy that pulses through every cell in your body. That energy is Essence, and it is always with you.

I wrote this book to help deepen our understanding and connection with the loving, wise, compassionate energy of goodness that is our true Essence and the Essence of all existence. I don't claim to be a guru or someone who has all the answers, but I've been fortunate enough to experience the truth of Essence and to feel its blessings. Like everyone, I forget my Essence frequently; I go through ups and downs just like my readers do. But when you've felt the truth and love that are inside our deepest core, when you've listened to your own inner voice and seen what can happen when you heed its advice, and when you've been uplifted in times of crisis by the sense that a love greater than anything in the universe is holding you in the palm of its hand, then you'll have an idea of what motivates me to write this book. In its pages, I hope you'll find truths that resonate with what you intuitively know inside, as well as ways to connect with Essence in your daily life, in your spiritual journey, in your relationships, in nature, and in moments of great joy and sorrow, including moments of death. In the New Testament, the Apostle John wrote, "The truth will set you free." I believe that when we understand the truth of our own Essence and live consciously from that knowledge, we are free to live, love, give, and walk through this world in greater happiness and fulfillment.

YOUR SOUL'S ENERGY BOOSTERS

- Our souls exist before we are born, and our spirits do not die when our bodies stop working.
- "Life is a school, we are here to learn lessons." "Cherish your loved ones every day." "Live in such a way that you will have no regrets." "You are part of something far greater than yourself." "You can tap in to the universal energy of goodness, wisdom, and love and use its guidance to prevent problems and guide your life."
- Our Essence is always there even when we're not aware of it, because it's all around us.
- When we connect with Essence, we remember that, while there is good and evil in this world, we are here to choose the good. Every time we choose good over

evil, we strengthen the presence of Essence in our lives. When we feel it, our lives are happier and more complete.

- It's called the law of karma: what you sow in one lifetime, you will reap in the next. Only when the past karma of evil deeds is atoned for can your soul continue its progress.
- Living in Essence shows us how to deal with fear, with crisis, with catastrophe. When we are connected with our inner truth and divinity, we can face our fears and either overcome them or use them as the warnings they are.
- Essence is joy, bliss, connectedness to everything. Essence is like the air you breathe—always present, rarely noticed, but essential for life.

TWO

The Qualities of Essence

He is the essence that inquires.
He is the axis of the star;
He is the sparkle of the spar;
He is the heart of every creature;
He is the meaning of each feature;
And his mind is the sky,
Than all it holds more deep, more high.

—RALPH WALDO EMERSON

There's a story of a seeker who came to a master in search of Essence. "You are enlightened, so you must know Essence," the seeker said. "Can you tell me what it is and how to recognize it?"

The master paused. How could he describe the indescribable? Then he said, "Describe the fragrance of a rose."

The seeker was silent.

Describing Essence is like trying to talk about falling in love with someone who has never had the experience. When you were younger, you probably heard many songs that talked about love and you just didn't get it. But the moment you fell in love, you knew exactly what you were experiencing, and all those songs and poems spoke directly to your heart. In the *Hua Hu Ching*, Lao-Tzu wrote of the Tao, "The only way to understand it is to directly experience it." There's a flicker of this experience available to you at any moment, if you allow it to surface. After you have the experience, you will move from *believing* in the possibility of being part of this universal energy to knowing for sure that it exists.

While the experience of Essence is almost impossible to describe, it does possess qualities that help us recognize these moments when they occur. These qualities are like signposts that help point us to a fuller awareness of Essence.

Essence Is Love

You are loved. If so, what else matters?

—EDNA ST. VINCENT MILLAY

Many people tell me, "Sure, I believe there's some sort of energy that makes up everything, but I can't believe that it's concerned about me in particular or even humankind in general." It can be tough to wrap your mind around the idea that Essence is everything and everyone, omnipresent and omnipotent, in every cell and molecule of your body, and yet it is also intelligent, loving, and wise. But once you have a direct experience of Essence, there's an incredibly personal feeling of an energy or presence that cares for and about *you*. As poet Richard Garnett wrote, "Love is God's essence; Power but his attribute: therefore is his love greater than his power." Essence is loving first and foremost. That's why I always say that it is your greatest friend.

Sometimes I think it's easier to connect to this personal, loving

Essence outside of ourselves rather than inside—in the same way that many of us find it easier to love others and to appreciate their great qualities long before we love ourselves. I think one of the reasons there is love here on Earth is so that we'll have a way of understanding and feeling Essence in a personal way. When we feel love for others, eventually, we'll recognize the love of which Essence is composed.

CONNECTING TO ESSENCE IN A LOVED ONE

Think of someone you love very much, whether he or she is living or on the other side. Close your eyes and call them to you. With all your heart, tell them, "I love you," and really mean it. Let your love vibrate inside for a few moments, and notice how you feel. Can you sense the presence of the other person even if they're not physically nearby? Can you feel the subtle energy of love inside yourself?

Love and our loving thoughts keep us connected both to Essence and to people on the other side. I saw a beautiful example of this when I read for Rob, a sweet, white-haired gentleman whom I met in a cemetery in Amsterdam. He was there to visit his parents' graves; he told me he brought fresh flowers every month. As soon as I spoke to Rob, I picked up on his father, Abraham, and his mother, Elizabeth. "Most of the time, I'm apologizing in readings, either for the people here or the spirits on the other side," I said. "But your relationship with your parents was always good, happy, and loving. Your parents loved you completely, and you loved them completely. There was no stone left unturned in your relationship. Now the spirits of your parents visit you at home, and they protect you and take good care of you."

Rob beamed. "I feel this, yes. They are with me all the time."

"You're very happy, and they're very happy you are their son," I said to him as I took his hand. This man radiated goodness, love, peace, and happiness. Just being with him, I could tell he was connected to Essence and to his loved ones on the other side.

I've also seen people who have been completely cut off from their Essence or their departed loved ones. Some individuals don't believe in Essence or life after death, and thus they ignore or discount any feeling they experience or message they receive. "The universe is an accident, and even if we're all composed of energy, it's completely impersonal," they say. "That light that went on and off was probably just a short circuit. Certainly it had nothing to do with a spirit trying to communicate with me." I've tried to read for some of these people, and it's truly sad. It feels as if they're cut off from themselves, from others, and from the gifts and joys of this world and the next. It's like a story I heard once of an unhappy monk who went to see the abbot of his monastery and asked, "Why is everyone here but me so happy?"

"Because your brother monks have learned to see goodness and beauty everywhere," the abbot replied.

"And why can't I see goodness and beauty?" the monk said, frustrated.

"Because you don't see it within yourself," answered the abbot gently.

Two men look out through the same bars;
One sees the mud, and one the stars.

—FREDERICK LANGBRIDGE

Other people feel so depressed or guilty or unhappy that their negative emotions completely block out any experience of the love of Essence or people on the other side (or often, here on Earth). I read for a family where the mother had passed away ten years earlier, and they were still grieving for her. The children and father all gathered around me, eager to hear from their departed dear one. Within moments, I gave them the names of all the grandchildren in the family. "Your mom is really happy about her grandkids!" I said. Then I gave them the name of the mother, Susanna. "She's telling me she's appeared to your children a couple of times. Did one of them tell you, 'Oma came to play with me'?"

The daughter gasped. "Yes! My daughter said she saw Oma in her room, wearing a white dress."

"Susanna is watching over her grandchildren and helping you, but she's saying you've got to stop being upset about her death," I told them firmly. "It's too hard on her in heaven. She tries to let you know that she's with you and gives you signs, but you don't always listen. She wants all of you to be happy and know that she's an angel watching over you in heaven."

It was as if the entire family sighed with relief. There were smiles and tears as they thanked me for helping their mother speak to them. Susanna had tried very hard to make her presence known to her family, but their grief was getting in the way. That's why it's often easier for departed spirits to speak to children—they have less emotional and psychological baggage that blocks the communication.

The energies of our loved ones can come through more clearly when our own negative emotional or psychological energy doesn't get in the way. The same is true of our awareness of Essence. Focusing on our problems, grief, or traumas can prevent us from hearing the still, small voice of Essence. That's one of the reasons I'm such a believer in getting psychological and emotional support and therapy. It's kind of like taking your car to the car wash after it's been through a major storm and it's covered with mud and debris from the trip. You can't move forward until you clean the windows and make sure there's no dirt in the engine. Once the car is clean inside and out, you can see the road ahead and resume your journey. In the same way, people may need to clean out their minds and emotions through counseling so they can see the truth of their own divine natures. None of us are in this alone; we can seek out and accept the help that's available here on Earth to process our emotions and heal our wounded psyches, so we can pay attention to our Essence and keep moving forward.

Essence Is Pure and Innocent

Blessed are the pure in heart, for they shall see God.

—MATTHEW 5:9

Howard K. Beattie once wrote, "Children, having spent more recent time on a spiritual level, remind adults of a timeless connection to the spiritual world and its love and wisdom." Babies are very close to Essence; their energy is innocent and uncluttered. That's why most of us respond emotionally when we're around them. Even when a baby is crying or fussing, our hearts go out to them and we want to help. A baby wants and needs our love, and it gives its own love purely and without conditions. It's the same with the young of almost every species. How do we respond when we see puppies or kittens? Even the young of ferocious animals like wolves, lions, or tigers can bring out feelings of love and protectiveness in us. Scientists may say that it's simply the "biological imperative" instinct for species survival that drives us to protect the young, but I believe it's something more. The quality of innocence and freshness that the young of any species possess is a reflection of the same quality of Essence.

CONNECTING TO ESSENCE IN A BABY

Imagine you're in a house, perhaps your own, perhaps the home of someone you know. You walk into one of the bedrooms and you see a crib with a baby inside, peacefully asleep. This baby is special to you in some way—it may be your child, or the child of a family member, or the child of your dearest friend. You walk over to the crib and look down at the baby. Notice the baby's soft skin, its downy hair, its chubby cheeks. Reach down and touch its hand gently, and feel its fingers curl around yours. Smell the sweet fragrance that only babies possess. The baby is breathing quietly, in and out. It's so innocent, peaceful, and happy. Say silently to the baby, "I love you," and really mean it. Can you feel the innocence and freshness of this new spirit?

Essence is reborn in every minute. It predates time yet is always new and fresh. It is also pure and uncluttered. A baby doesn't care if you have a lot of money in the bank or just left your latest relationship. It simply exists to love and be loved. Its innocence and freshness make us all feel new and young again. And when we see Essence in a baby, we can feel Essence in ourselves.

Essence Is Truth

Great is truth, and mighty above all things.

—1 ESDRAS 4:41, APOCRYPHA

In Zen Buddhism, masters use koans, questions that would seem to have no logical answer, to get their students to think beyond the surface. The goal is for the students to experience a flash of insight, a glimpse of a deeper level of truth. In this moment, a student can attain enlightenment, or a complete awareness of Essence. While I am certainly no master of any kind, I've seen the same flash of insight in people during readings when they hear a piece of information that only a departed loved one would know being communicated through me. Thom, whom you met in chapter 1, had that flash of insight when I told him about the picture he had placed on his wife's heart right before she was cremated. No one knew about that picture but him and his wife. I also saw that flash of insight when I read for a woman who had lost her mother several years earlier. The mother had wanted her daughter to have children, but she got sick before the daughter became pregnant. Nevertheless, the mother bought baby clothes for the child she intuitively knew her daughter would have. I picked up on all this, and then I told the daughter, "Your mom is showing me a blanket. Did she make a blanket for your child?"

The daughter looked at me in shock. "She made a blanket for my cousin's baby, and when I had my child, my cousin gave the blanket to me. No one knew that but my cousin and me." Later she sent me a picture of the beautiful blanket her mother had made. With that detail and the other clear communications from her mom during the course of the reading, the daughter saw the truth of life beyond death for the first time and knew that her mother on the other side was celebrating the grandchild she had prepared for with such joy.

The gift of truth is the highest gift.
The taste of truth is the sweetest taste.
The joy of truth is the greatest joy.

—THE DHAMMAPADA: THE PATH OF TRUTH

There are moments in our lives where we think and believe that something is true, and other moments when we simply know that we have heard or seen or are experiencing an Essential Truth. This is not the same as the feeling of "I'm right, and they're wrong." That's usually self-righteousness, and it comes not from Essence but from the ego's need to feed its sense of importance. The truth of Essence is usually very humble yet clear. As the philosopher Blaise Pascal wrote, "We know the truth, not only by the reason, but also by the heart." Essential truth unites us rather than divides us. It shows us how we are all part of Essence instead of separating us into good and bad, right and wrong, even enlightened and unenlightened. Like the experience of a student who sees the truth behind an unanswered question, truth unites us with itself in a flash, not just of understanding but of *knowing*. In those moments, our doubts about the existence of Essence or life after death completely disappear. We know and feel the truth of our own eternal nature.

Essence Is Holy

A true love of God must begin with a delight in his holiness.

—JONATHAN EDWARDS, SEVENTEENTH-CENTURY MINISTER

Holiness doesn't mean holier-than-thou, or feeling like someone else is better than we are. Holiness is simply an awareness of a deep and direct connection with something good and wise, something far greater than one individual's experience. "How little people know who think that holiness is dull. When one meets the real thing . . . it is irresistible," wrote C. S. Lewis. When we're around people who are holy, we often can tell simply by the way they make us feel. Great beings like the Buddha and Jesus, saints like Francis and Teresa, Zen masters like Bodhidharma, or Sufi saints like

Rumi and Hafiz, had this quality. Just by being in their presence, people felt connected to Essence. And reading about them and reading their words can help us connect to our Essence as well. There are many terms for this state of being one with Essence. Some traditions call it *enlightenment.* Others call it *awakened,* or *mindful,* or *Oneness,* or *being with God.* In the Jewish and Christian traditions, we call it *holy.* In this state, there is no sense of division between our small self and the big Self with a capital *S.* We are connected completely to Essence at every moment. Recognizing this place of peace is the ultimate secret to life.

The irony is that all these great and holy masters are pointing us to the very simple truth that each of us is holy, each of us is Essence, and all we need to do is become aware of this truth. There's a story of a sage who drew to herself thousands of seekers because of her clear and tangible connection with Essence. She would shake her head and say with a chuckle, "All I do is sit by the bank of the river, selling river water." The river lies in each of us, if we but knew enough to dip our cup into the holiness within.

The other mistake that many of us make when we sense Essence in someone else is to think that they have it and we don't. We try to turn our teachers into gods or gurus. We believe that somehow, they are different from or better than we are. As the sages say, we mistake the finger pointing at the moon for the moon itself. We turn our teachers into false idols because it's easier to worship them and think they've "got it" and they can intercede for us, rather than take on the awesome responsibility of recognizing that we ourselves are just as holy as they are. To quote Marianne Williamson: "Our deepest fear is not that we are inadequate. Our deepest fear is that we are powerful beyond measure. It is our light, not our darkness, that most frightens us. We ask ourselves, Who am I to be brilliant, gorgeous, talented, fabulous? Actually, who are you *not* to be? . . . We were born to make manifest the glory of God that is within us. It's not just in some of us; it's in everyone." We each contain the holiness of Essence, and we have the responsibility to recognize it and make it manifest in the world.

Essence Is in the Present Moment

When you are present, when your attention is fully and intensely in the Now, Being can be felt. . . .

—ECKHART TOLLE, *THE POWER OF NOW*

Essence contains all time, past, present, and future; but it can be experienced only in the present, in what Eckhart Tolle and many other teachers call the Now. In the present are emotions like love, joy, peace, happiness, even enlightenment. When you're fully in the present, there is no stress; if you focus on the Now, there's no past or future, so what is there to be stressed about? When we experience the present moment fully, the mind stops its endless chatter and we can just *be.* Vipassana, a type of meditation practiced since the time of the Buddha in 500 B.C., is based on focusing attention on the present moment and experiencing what is.

CONNECTING TO ESSENCE IN THE PRESENT MOMENT

Sit comfortably in a quiet place. Close your eyes and start to notice everything you hear. Let yourself become fully aware of the sounds in your environment. Don't try to interpret the noises;

simply notice them. Then become aware of the sensations in your body—how your skin feels next to your clothes, the weight of your body on the chair, any tension you may experience. Notice without trying to change the feelings in any way.

Now, turn your attention to your breath as it comes in and goes out. Again, simply notice it; don't try to alter it in any way. If you notice your thoughts, tell yourself, It's the nature of the mind to think, and let them go as you gently focus on your breath again. There is nothing but the breath, nothing but the present moment. Let yourself relax into the Now.

You may or may not find it easy to let your thoughts go. Like most people, I have a mind that goes ninety miles a minute and is active most of the time. I often find myself caught up thinking about the past or worrying about the future. But when I do readings, I have to drop all thoughts of past and future and focus intensely on what I'm receiving in the present moment. The thoughts, feelings, and impressions that come in my readings arise directly from being fully in the present. In a way, readings for me are a form of meditation where I connect to Essence in the present moment and thus can connect to energies both here and on the other side.

Essence Is Lighthearted

Time spent laughing is time spent with the Gods.

—JAPANESE PROVERB

Most religious traditions teach us that it is a long and difficult journey to reach the state of oneness with Essence—even though it's actually who we are! That's really the biggest cosmic joke of all, and I think it's the reason that so many great beings possess such lightness. They know that Essence has a sense of humor. Anytime we're touching into Essence, laughter and lightness can arise. Even the holy beings who can awaken us to our own Essence are not "holy" in the sense of being solemn and forbidding. Indeed, they call us to dance and sing and rejoice, or at the very least, to see how silly our concepts and pretensions and efforts have been.

I find it's the same thing with people who have passed over—they're happy and filled with joy and lightness on the other side. Not too long ago, I did a reading for a family whom I met in a local memorial park. The wife of the oldest gentleman in the group came through immediately. "She's dancing on the other side—she liked to dance, right?" I told them. "She's young again, and she's telling me that when you come to heaven, you'd better be ready to dance with her!" Most of our loved ones are happy and whole again after death, and they're joyously waiting for us to join them when it's our time. And one of the reasons our loved ones are so happy is that they are living in the awareness of their Essence and its lighthearted, expansive, loving energy.

When we connect with this inner energy, we naturally want to celebrate and dance. It's this energy that the author of Psalm 100 describes when he directs us to "make a joyful noise unto the Lord, all ye lands. Serve the Lord with gladness: come before his presence with singing. . . . Enter into his gates with thanksgiving, and into his courts with praise." Or as the fifteenth-century Indian saint Kabir wrote: "Dance, my heart! dance to-day with joy. / The strains of love fill the days and the nights with music, and the world is listening to its melodies: / Mad with joy, life and death dance to the rhythm of this music. . . . / Behold! my heart dances in the delight of a hundred arts; and the Creator is well pleased."

Essence Is Peaceful and Content

The peace of God, which passeth all understanding . . .

—*THE BOOK OF COMMON PRAYER*, 1928

Not too long ago, I did a reading for a lovely young girl. "Do you have an *M,* deceased—Mathilda? Is this your grandmother?" The girl nodded, wide-eyed. "I see a little girl in bed, I think it's you, and Mathilda is putting blankets on you and kissing you good night. She was the one who loved you the most. She's wearing a dress with flowers on it—she wore this all the time, right?"

The girl smiled. "She loved colors. Is my grandmother okay?"

"She's more than okay," I told her. "I feel that she's really peaceful. Did she have a difficult time with one of her children?"

"My mother," the girl replied.

"Well, your grandma's in a place where she has even more peace and happiness than when she was here. She loves you and appreciates all you did for her. She's an angel watching over you all the time."

Peace is one of the clearest emotional confirmations that we are at one with Essence, either here or in spirit. This kind of peace is not simply the absence of worry, or conflict, or the resolution of a dispute. It is a deep feeling that "all will be well, and all will be well, and all manner of things will be well," as the mystic Julian of Norwich wrote. Often when we meditate, the experience of peace lets us know that we have touched Essence. These feelings of peace and contentment may have nothing to do with our outer circumstances. In fact, it's when our outer circumstances are troubled and tumultuous that we notice most the peace and contentment that emanates from Essence, simply because it's the only place it could come from.

Have you ever watched a truly great martial artist? Their movements arise not from physical power but from a deep, still center of calm. A great martial arts master is connected with the energy of Essence and draws his or her power from there. In the same way, we can draw enormous power and resourcefulness in the toughest circumstances by turning within and touching the peace and contentment of Essence that is always present. The next time you are in a stressful situation, take a moment and turn your focus away from what's happening and toward the inner core of your being. Say a prayer and ask for peace and contentment no matter what the outside circumstances. Allow yourself to become quiet, and notice the feelings inside. You may find peace and contentment when you least expect it—and when you need it most.

Essence Is Within You

Closer is He than breathing,
and nearer than hands and feet.

—ALFRED, LORD TENNYSON

There's a story that when Adam and Eve were cast out of the Garden of Eden, God decided he wanted to put his Essence somewhere that human beings would take a long time to find. "Give it to me!" said the fish. "I'll swim with it down to the deepest part of the ocean. They'll never swim that far."

"Give it to me!" said the mole. "I'll bury it in the remotest cave in the world. Humans will never reach it."

"No, give it to me!" said the eagle. "I'll fly with it to the top of the tallest mountain. No one can climb that high."

God smiled at his creatures. "Thank you for your offers, but I plan to hide my Essence in the heart of every human being. They'll never look there!"

Humankind has spent lifetime after lifetime "looking for love in all the wrong places," as the old song goes. We have tried to turn almost everything, from nature to relationships to science to technology into the latest version of God, and never looked inside ourselves. That's because it's a lot easier to put God "out there" than it is to see God inside.

CONNECTING TO ESSENCE IN YOURSELF

Go back to the exercise Connecting to Essence in a Loved One and connect to the person you love the most in the world. Re-establish that loving feeling inside of you. Now, imagine that instead of your loved one you see yourself, standing about a meter away. Look into your own eyes and, with all your heart, say, "I love you," and really mean it. See yourself smiling and receiving your love. Is this feeling of love the same as it was in Exercise #1, or is it different? Do you find it harder to love yourself than you do others? If so, try saying to yourself, "I love you with all your flaws and your good qualities. You are perfect just as you are," and really mean it. See what happens to the feelings in your heart.

Every experience we have of Essence in the outside world—whether it comes from the loving glance of a child or parent or spouse, or from being immersed in the glories of nature, or from studying the words of masters who point us toward the truth—ultimately must drive us inward. Love, nature, and learning are merely fingers pointing at the "moon" of our inner world. That is the only place where we can truly *experience* the qualities of Essence.

I heard a story about a lover of God who longed for union with Essence. After years of study and meditation, one night he dreamed he was at the door of the house of the Lord. He knocked, and he heard God ask, "Who is it?"

"It is I," the lover said.

"Go away," the voice replied. "This house is not big enough for us both."

The lover of God awoke from the dream, heartbroken. He went into the wilderness where he meditated for days on end and sought to understand what God had meant. Finally, a night came where he dreamed once more of the house of the Lord. With trembling hands, he knocked again.

"Who is it?" the voice asked.

"It is you," the lover of God answered.

Immediately, the door opened.

Are you ready to knock on the door and be welcomed by your Essence?

YOUR SOUL'S ENERGY BOOSTERS

- After you have the experience of connecting to Essence you will move from believing in the possibility to knowing for sure that it exists.
- I use the word Essence to describe the fundamental, living, intelligent, loving energy that makes up the entire universe and everything beyond it.

- The energies of our loved ones can come through more clearly when our own negative emotional or psychological energy doesn't get in the way. The same is true of our awareness with Essence. Focusing on our problems, grief, or traumas can prevent us from hearing the still, small voice of Essence.
- Essence is pure and innocent.
- Essence is truth; we know it and feel it.
- Essence is holy; we are all holy and can manifest it.
- Essence is the present moment; experience it fully.
- Essence is lighthearted and has a sense of humor.
- Essence is peaceful and content even in times of chaos, stress, and turmoil.
- Essence is within you. Look in the mirror and say, "I love you, despite any imperfections."

THREE

Listening to Essence

When you become quiet, it just dawns on you.

—THOMAS EDISON

Do you have a voice inside your head that just never shuts up? The one that comments on anything and everything and sometimes keeps you awake at night with worry? Many of the traditions that teach meditation call this chatterbox *monkey mind,* because its energy feels as frantic and as scattered as a monkey swinging through the trees. Monkey mind's focus is rarely on the present moment; it's always bringing up references from the past or creating dreams or plans or worries about the future. When you listen to the stream of consciousness that is your monkey mind, even though the thoughts are familiar, they can cause you to feel unsettled, upset, and tense.

That's not the inner voice I'm speaking of when I say, "Listen to Essence." In fact, that incessantly commenting chatterbox is the part of the conscious mind that actually gets in the way of our true inner wisdom—the voice of knowingness that is your intuition. Always remember, the universe is calling you. When we can quiet the monkey mind, we can open ourselves to connect to wisdom that goes beyond our own limited experience. We can link ourselves to the great net that makes up the universe and be receptive to the information that Essence wants to give us. We also can ask the questions that will help us grow, prevent problems, and attain goals.

Intuition is one of the best channels of communication between the conscious mind and Essence. Part of my mission has always been to awaken people to their inborn, intuitive power and to teach them how to listen to their sixth sense. Like our other senses, intuition is both God-given and a valuable asset in making our way in the world. But unlike the five other senses, intuition can connect us directly to Essence. When we use our intuition, we must clear our inner obstacles and acknowledge an infinite force that is beyond our own limited experience. Intuition can help us forge a link between our spirit and all that is. It can bring the energy of Essence to our everyday consciousness. And as I discuss in my book *Discover Your Inner Wisdom,* when intuition is combined with the conscious forces of logic and common sense, we have a powerful guide for our actions.

The "Voice" of Essence

We lie in the lap of an immense
intelligence and we are receptors.

—RALPH WALDO EMERSON

While I call it an inner "voice," the guidance we receive from Essence can come in many different forms and through all of our senses. You could be sitting at home and all of a sudden you notice a family photo of you and your brother, Peter. Somehow Peter's face seems brighter than the others in the photo, and a thought pops into your head: *Peter's going to have a son.* You call your brother, who tells you that he and his wife are expecting a baby. Or you're listening to the radio on the way home from work and you hear the announcer say, "A study released today reveals that 50 percent of automobile accidents are caused by people running red lights." Somehow this statistic sticks in your mind. Five minutes later, you are stopped at a red light. It turns green, but you wait a second before stepping on the gas—and you just miss getting hit by a driver who runs the red light. Our intuitive voice can show up in different smells as well. A friend of mine says that if she smells her grandmother's perfume when she meets someone, she knows they will be trustworthy. (She will smell this fragrance whether the person is wearing it or not.) The inner voice of intuition also manifests as emotions that seemingly come from nowhere. You may feel peace and content, a "knowingness," for instance, when embarking on a new venture that ends up being a success. Or you may feel a sense of foreboding or unhappiness when you're around someone who turns out to be bad for you. Or you might get an uneasy sensation in your heart or stomach—the original gut instinct—when presented with an investment opportunity. You say no, and you find out later that the investors lost all their money.

Sometimes your inner voice speaks without your asking it anything. It may tell you to apply for a particular job, or to invest in a friend's business venture. Perhaps it's a warning not to take a certain plane or train, or to stay away from someone at work. These moments of spontaneous communication are gifts from Essence designed to guide us in our life choices. We ignore these intuitive flashes at our peril. Granted, Essence is not going to warn us about everything bad that might happen to us. If it did, we would miss out on a lot of the lessons we've come to Earth to learn. But if Essence thinks it's important enough to warn us or give us the go-ahead, we'd be smart to take its advice.

While Essence can use any means it chooses to get important messages across, our inner voice often uses a particular vehicle—sight, sound, taste, touch, emotions, and so on—to communicate. You may want to write down the occasions when what your inner voice said came true, as they may be indications of the particular ways Essence chooses to speak to you.

WHEN DID YOU LISTEN TO ESSENCE?

Remember a time when you received a message that simply couldn't have come from your conscious mind. Maybe it was a feeling that something was wrong with a loved one. Maybe you saw or heard something that helped you avoid a potential problem or take advantage of an opportunity. Perhaps it was a gut feeling that turned out to be accurate. Perhaps it was a time when for no particular reason you thought of someone and the next minute, they telephoned. Acknowledging messages from Essence will help us notice the next one that comes along.

Essence also speaks to us through coincidences. You are debating whether or not to get a dog. The next day, you get a postcard from the local shelter saying, "Pet adoptions Saturday!" and on the front is the picture of the exact kind of dog you'd always pictured owning. Then out of the blue, your coworker tells you a story about the dog he owned for fifteen years. Finally, your next-door neighbor knocks on your door. "I'm cleaning out my closets and found a lot of stuff that belonged to our dog that died," she says. "Do you know anyone who could use this?" You think, *Okay, I get the message!* You go to the shelter on Saturday and there is the perfect dog for you—the exact breed, age, and personality. While this may seem like an extreme example, I've heard of many people who have experienced similar runs of "coincidence." The secret, of course, is to be receptive to the promptings of Essence, acknowledge the fact that these coincidences are signs, not just accidents, and then take action on what Essence is telling us. (We'll speak more of this in chapter 4.)

At times, Essence chooses to speak to us through our dreams. Dreams get past the barriers and skepticism of the conscious mind and tap directly into the other-than-conscious part of our brains. Dreams allow us to work on problems that we can't face otherwise, and more important, they allow information that does not come from the conscious mind to present itself. Our departed loved ones often come to us in dreams because it's easier for them to communicate in this way. But Essence also can use dreams to give us information, direction, and guidance. Many people who come to me for readings will tell me that they dreamed of their loved one's death before it actually occurred. Not too long ago, I dreamed that two of my good friends, who had been together for twelve years, broke up. At the time, I laughed it off, but six months later, my friends ended their relationship.

It's good to capture such dreams so you can use their guidance. Some psychic dreams will "feel" different and can be easily recognized. Others, like the dream about my friends, may seem inconsequential at the time but prove true later. I like to keep a notebook and pen by my bedside to jot down any dreams I remember when I wake. Dreams can be a source of clear communication from Essence, and when their guidance is combined with logic, common sense, and gut instinct, they can help us prevent problems and shape our future.

Asking Questions of Essence

Intuitive intelligence is more accurate and precise than anything that exists in the realm of rational thought.

—DEEPAK CHOPRA

Rather than simply waiting for our inner voice to speak up, we can ask Essence to communicate with us directly. Essence wants to offer guidance in many situations, and by giving it an opportunity to be heard, we not only can make our lives easier and encounter fewer problems, we also can develop the habit of listening to what Essence wants to tell us and thus create a stronger, easier, more natural connection with our own inner divine nature. In *Discover Your Inner Wisdom,* I described a simple method of asking questions of Essence using your intuitive sixth sense. You are welcome to try this yourself, especially if you feel you need guidance in a particular area or if you would just like to learn to listen more closely to the whispers of direction that Essence wants to give.

STEP 1: CREATE A SPECIFIC AND CLEAR QUESTION.

Asking for guidance is like asking for directions: the more specific your question, the clearer the answer is likely to be. "Will I meet my soul mate?" is too general. The answer may be yes—but you may not meet that person in this lifetime. "Should I take this job?" or "Should I buy this house?" or "Is my spouse cheating on me?" or "Is this school going to be good for my child?" are examples of specific questions. The clearer your question, the easier it will be for you to discover and understand the answer you receive.

STEP 2: PREPARE TO RECEIVE WHAT ESSENCE HAS TO GIVE.

Intuitive asking requires your full attention, so you stand a better chance of hearing what Essence has to say if you focus completely. Set aside a specific time to ask your question. Turn off your phone, iPad, computer, and any other device that might interrupt you. Find a calm, peaceful, and comfortable environment. If you have a particular spot where you like to meditate, that's a great place for this process, as you are used to tuning in to Essence there. I suggest that you have paper and pen handy to capture any thoughts, feelings, or impressions you may receive.

Sit down and make yourself comfortable. If there is some ritual you do before you meditate—lighting a candle, repeating a mantra—you can do that now. Next, close your eyes, envision in your mind a bright white light that comes from the depth of your soul and illuminates to the outside of your body as if you are radiating light like the sun. Say a prayer to protect you from any negative energies and to ensure that the messages you receive come from Essence. As we'll discuss in later chapters, while Essence wants only what is good for us, there are other, lower energies that like to trick or even harm us. Surrounding yourself with white light and saying a prayer of protection is like tuning yourself to the proper channel to receive only the highest and best communication.

STEP 3: CLEAR YOUR MIND OF THOUGHTS AND FOCUS ON THE PRESENT.

Take a few deep breaths, and then turn your focus inside. If you meditate, use whatever technique you find effective to clear your mind and calm your thoughts. Breathe gently in and out. Put all desires and wishes aside and be open to whatever you receive. Bring your focus completely to the moment. Let your thoughts, your emotions, your wishes, your desires come and go like your breath. Become completely centered, balanced, and relaxed in the present moment.

STEP 4: ASK YOUR QUESTION WITHOUT BEING EMOTIONALLY INVOLVED.

In this connected state, ask your question. Ideally, you should ask without any hint of emotional attachment to a specific reply. (While desires and wishes are important in manifestation, they also can block the subtle energies of Essence from communicating clearly with us.) Remember, Essence wants what is best for us, even if it doesn't always seem so. When you ask your question, you must trust that whatever answer you receive will be for your highest good and greatest growth.

STEP 5: PAY ATTENTION TO WHAT YOU'RE GETTING.

With intuitive asking, you want to pay attention to thoughts that come from somewhere beyond the conscious mind. Make note of the first thought that comes into your head that feels as if it is not a conscious response. Use your notebook to jot down any impressions. Make notes of exactly what you receive—images, sounds, feelings—and don't edit or try to explain. Interpretation can come later; for now, you want simply to notice what comes up. Sometimes your answer will be a clear yes or no, or it could be a positive or negative feeling. Your answer also could come in the form of a symbol. For example, you ask if you will be in a romantic relationship within the year, and inside your mind you see a bridal bouquet. Or you ask about your current job and you hear the sound of a door slamming, which you interpret as a sign that your time there is done and you need to look for another position.

Your answer may not come immediately, or it may show up when you're not thinking about your question at all—perhaps as you go to sleep or wake up. Or it may appear as a feeling of certainty that grows over the next few hours or days. Be patient, stay alert, and trust that you will receive your answer—if you are meant to have one. We aren't meant to have answers to all our questions; if we did, we couldn't get the lessons we're supposed to learn. It's also possible that the circumstances around your question are unsettled. Past, present, and future all exist within Essence, but the future is constantly being reshaped by events and our choices, as well as the choices of others. For example, you're offered a promotion at work, but you're unsure whether to take it. You ask Essence for guidance and receive no indication either way. A month later, you find out you (or your spouse) are pregnant. Do you take the new job because it will mean more income for your growing family? Do you turn it down and stay at your current job so you can focus on preparing for a new baby? Or do you leave work altogether and become a stay-at-home parent? All of these options will affect the new job opportunity, so it's no wonder your question went unanswered. Whenever there's no reply from Essence, you may need to trust that the answer will become clear as future events unfold.

You also have to be willing for the answer to be different from your desires. Sometimes we ask our inner voice and Essence for guidance, but what we're really looking for is validation. Being open means being willing to hear and accept whatever answer Essence provides, and to be emotionally neutral about the reply. Emotions and desires can get in our way if they go against the natural flow of universal energy. When asking questions of Essence, your desire must be to align yourself with what Essence wants for you; your belief must be that it will bring to you exactly what you want and need for your benefit and growth.

Finally, you must remember that Essence has given you other tools to help you make decisions and guide your life. Those tools include logic and common sense, and they must be part of any decision you make. Essence is also present in our conscious mind and in the wisdom accumulated through experience and learning. Intuition can take you places logic and common sense never will, but when you combine logic, common sense, and intuition, you'll make wiser choices. Allow Essence to speak to you through all three.

STEP 6: FOLLOW THE GUIDANCE YOU'VE RECEIVED.

Essence guides but doesn't do the work for us; that's our job. As a Russian proverb says, "Pray to God but continue to row to shore." We come to Earth to make choices, learn from them, and to grow in love and wisdom from these lessons. If we're smart, we ask Essence for its guidance and heed its answers to shape our actions. When we learn to listen for the subtle promptings of Essence, we move within the flow of the universe rather than trying to swim against the tide.

Connecting to Essence Through Prayer

More things are wrought by prayer
Than this world dreams of.

—ALFRED, LORD TENNYSON

On many weekdays, my father would leave our house very early to go to the local synagogue before work. In the Jewish faith, we say prayers for the dead during the first year after someone passes over. But there needs to be a minyan, a minimum of seven people, to say the prayers in temple. So my dad would go to synagogue to be sure there were enough participants for a minyan so the prayers for the dead could be recited. He did this for people he didn't even know. Talk about a mitzvah—a good deed. Throughout my childhood, both my parents taught me the power and importance of prayer. When we pray, we focus our awareness on the source of goodness, wisdom, and love of which we are part. Every spiritual tradition incorporates prayer as one of its most important practices. Devoted Muslims pray five times every day. Christians recite the Lord's Prayer and, if they are Catholic, the rosary. Hindus recite prayers in the ancient language of Sanskrit. Buddhists spin prayer wheels and repeat the many names of God. Prayer uses the power of our thoughts and awareness to remind us that we are part of, and guided by, the divine. When we pray, we are recognizing that there is something outside our own limited experience that cares for us. As we connect with the divine energy of Essence, we can feel the resonance of that same energy inside of us.

Prayers and loving thoughts are our connection not only to Essence but also to the people we care about both here and on the other side. Our prayers are some of the greatest gifts we can offer to our loved ones. In the same way that prayer elevates our energy, its positive power reaches spirits on the other side, letting them know of our love and helping them to heal any hurts and make progress more quickly. Whether your prayers are formal, as in saying the kaddish or the rosary or the Prayers for the Dead, or informal, loving thoughts, your prayer energy will connect you and the spirits of your departed dear ones.

Prayer can be an incredibly powerful force. The Old Testament tells the story of Daniel, who prayed to God three times a day and was thrown into the lions' den by King Darius because of it. But Daniel continued to pray, and God sent an angel to keep the lions from killing him. Most of the miracles described in the Bible are the result of the power of prayer. Indeed, one of the main criteria for recognizing someone as a saint in the Catholic tradition is a documented miracle as a result of someone praying to that particular saint to intercede for them in heaven. Even science is starting to recognize the power of prayer and directed thought. There are medical studies about the effects of prayer on people who are suffering from a variety of illnesses. Those who are prayed for often heal better and faster, even if they are unaware that they are being prayed for. Over and over, we hear about individuals facing death who make miraculous and speedy recoveries that doctors cannot explain and whose recovery may well be due to the power of prayer. Many people also report they could feel the energy of others' prayers supporting them in getting better.

Prayer can even help the environment. Masaru Emoto, a Japanese researcher who has shown the positive effects of words like *love* and *gratitude* on molecules of water, described an occasion in 1999 when a Shinto priest gathered a group of 350 people to go to Lake Biwa, one of the most polluted lakes in Japan. For several hours, this group stood by the lake and prayed. A month later, newspapers reported that the algae that appeared every year on Lake Biwa, fouling the water and creating a horrific stench, had not shown up at its usual time. The lake was free of the algae blight that year. There was no discernible reason for this change, other than the power of prayer.

There are as many different reasons for prayer as there are people. There are prayers of thanksgiving. Prayers that ask for help. Prayers during tough times. Prayers of praise. Prayers in remembrance of others. Prayers that ask for blessings on those we love. Prayers that ask for victory. Prayers for peace. Prayers that say, "Please let things turn out this way." Prayers that say, "Thy will be done." Prayers when we're at the end of our rope. Prayers that are conversations with the divine. Prayers to start or end the day. Prayer doesn't even require that we feel a strong connection with Essence. Some of the most profound prayers have come from the saints experiencing what Saint John of the Cross called "the dark night of the soul." I read not too long ago that Saint Mother Teresa spent years feeling that God wasn't listening to her prayers—yet she continued to pray and to minister to the dying. There are times in most of our lives where we feel cut off from our divine Essence, both inside and outside. That doesn't mean that Essence has ceased to exist, and it doesn't mean that we cease to be a part of it. Maybe it's a test of our faith to go through such periods. Maybe we need to learn to listen in a different way to the whispers of Essence. Maybe Essence is showing us we have everything we need inside. I don't know the reason for the "dark night of the soul," but I do know that in such times I don't stop praying, and neither should you. I've seen far too many people who have suffered tragedies in their lives and it has been the power of prayer—their own or the prayers of others—that has pulled them back into life. So if you find yourself feeling cut off from Essence, keep praying. If you put out the call, God will answer. Even if you can't hear Essence speaking to you, the line is still open.

> Hold your face up to the light, even though
> for the moment you do not see.
>
> —BILL WILSON, COFOUNDER, ALCOHOLICS ANONYMOUS

I'm certainly not presumptuous enough to teach anyone how to pray. What you do to connect with Essence is a matter between you and the divine. I will say, however, that you should be aware that prayer opens you to the energies of the universe, and you want to make sure that you connect with the highest energies. I start every reading by surrounding myself with white light and saying a prayer of protection. When you pray, make sure you are invoking the highest and asking for its attention and guidance. I also believe that prayer requires focus. Don't let your thoughts wander. If you find yourself getting distracted, do whatever you need to refocus on your connection with Essence. When you are seeking to talk to the highest, your thoughts have enormous power, and you need to keep them pointed toward Essence. Often, the best place to start a prayer is with gratitude. Love and gratitude create a vibration in the spirit that is naturally attuned to Essence.

Mahatma Gandhi once wrote, "It is better in prayer to have a heart without words, than words without heart." Whatever prayer you feel called upon to make, pray with your heart and not just with your mouth. Your prayer doesn't have to be beautiful or poetic—simply heartfelt. If you're more comfortable with familiar prayers, like the Lord's Prayer or the rosary, or prayers of your own faith tradition, by all means, repeat those. As long as you put your heart into them, the words can help you connect with the divine. It's also fine to pray without words. Focus your heart and mind on the goodness, wisdom, and love of Essence. Feel the gratitude inside your heart. Let yourself merge into the love that is your own inner nature and also makes up the universe, a love that is personal and yet everywhere.

Ideally, prayer is a two-way conversation: we offer thanks, share our thoughts with God, and then wait silently for God's response. The key word here is *listen*. How many of us have done a lot of praying where we told God exactly what was going on, complained about this and that, asked again and again for what we wanted—and never bothered to shut up and listen to what God may have wanted to say? Saint Mother Teresa wrote, "Prayer is not asking. Prayer is putting oneself in the hands of God, at his disposition, and listening to his voice in the depths of our hearts." In prayer, we open ourselves to the guidance of Essence. When we listen to its promptings, whether in prayer, or by asking our intuition, or by noticing the subtle promptings that appear in our everyday life, we can keep ourselves on the path of greatest growth, love, and happiness. We will recognize that Essence is with us and *is* us, always.

YOUR SOUL'S ENERGY BOOSTERS

- Intuition is one of the best channels of communication between the conscious mind and Essence. It comes at times as a gut feeling; listen to it and act upon it.

- When intuition is combined with the conscious forces of logic and common sense, we have a powerful guide for our actions.
- While Essence can use any means it chooses to get important messages across, our inner voice often uses a particular vehicle—sight, sound, taste, touch, emotions, and so on—to communicate.
- Essence speaks to us through coincidences and dreams. They can help us prevent problems and shape our future.
- Intuitive asking requires your full attention. We have the power to ask questions of Essence and to get answers.
- Prayers and loving thoughts are our connection not only to Essence, but also to the people we care about here and on the other side.
- Prayer can be an incredibly powerful healing force.

FOUR

Manifesting and Essence

Ask, and it shall be given to you; seek, and ye shall find; knock, and it shall be opened unto you.

—MATTHEW 7:7

Manifesting—turning dreams into reality—is a natural part of the human experience. In manifesting, we tap into the power of Essence to bring the unseen into physical form. Because we are all made from the same energy as Essence, its creative power is part of us. As Deepak Chopra put it, "If you really understood that who you are is the same field of intelligence that creates the body, the mind, and the entire cosmos . . . then why would you *not* have the power to manifest?"

When I was very young, I had a wish board—a bulletin board where I put pictures and words that represented things that I wanted to create in my life. Then I stopped using a board, until my friend Chantal mentioned her own dream board and how effective it was. Since then, I've put together an updated wish board every year. Most of my television shows were on my wish board long before the opportunities were offered to me. I put on the board the names of specific shows I wanted to be on (like *Today* and *Dr. Oz*) and pictures of the hosts as well. I wrote that my television series in the Netherlands would be highly rated in its time slot—and it was for ten straight seasons. Each of my books has been on my wish board long before they came out in print. And I've had a romance come true after I put the description of my boyfriend on the board. A wish board helps me visualize what I want and keeps my dreams in focus. It also helps me notice when I receive those little "assists" from Essence that tell me I'm on the right track. I think about the items on my wish board almost every day, and usually within six months to a year the wish will show up in my life. The energy of Essence is abundant, inexhaustible, and magnanimous, and tools like a wish board can help us use our thoughts, emotions, and will to connect to that energy and move it to act in our behalf.

A wish board links goal-setting and taking action with the energetic aspect of manifestation described in the law of attraction. The law of attraction states, "Whatever you focus on consistently, you will attract into your life." I am confident in our power to manifest our desires by focusing on them, but some of the things that have been said about the law of attraction have caused people to beat themselves up if they are not able to manifest their dreams. I believe that there are two important factors when it comes to putting the law of attraction to work in our lives. First, for us to manifest something, *the desire needs to be in alignment with what Essence wants for us*. That job you want so much? Maybe it's not the right career path for you. That relationship you can't live without? Essence may have other ideas, or there may be a better relationship around the corner. If you didn't manage to manifest that job or relationship, it may not be because you didn't try hard enough, or you didn't have a clear enough intention, or any of the thousand reasons you can use to feel bad about yourself. It could simply be that your goal wasn't a part of Essence's plan. We need to partner with Essence to discover what will be best for us instead of assuming that just because we want something, it means we're destined to have it. Remember, life is a school, and our primary purpose on Earth is to learn the lessons that will give us the greatest growth. Your greatest growth may come from *not* attaining your goal, or from reaching your goal and having it not pan out, or going after and attaining a different goal. Some of the greatest discoveries in science have come because someone failed to achieve what they desired, but along the way they discovered something far more important. We must trust that Essence always knows what's for our greatest benefit. Whenever we use the power of desire and intention, we must seek to know what Essence's will is for us.

Second, while each of us is an equal manifestation of the energy of Essence on Earth, *we are not the only ones involved in the creation of our desires*. We are part of an interconnected web of energy, and our every goal, intention, and desire intersect with the goals, intentions, and desires of others. When we set out to manifest our desires, we must take into account the currents of universal energy in play. That job you want may need to go to a parent of five so they can feed their family. The house you lose out on may be destined to burn down next year, and you're being saved from enormous heartache and loss. That's why it's so important to tap into Essence as part of the process of manifestation, to seek its guidance, and then flow with its energy rather than against it.

One of the first ways to attune yourself to Essence's role in manifestation is to see where it already has helped you create something.

WHAT HAS ESSENCE ALREADY HELPED YOU MANIFEST?

Draw three columns on a piece of paper. In the first column, make a list of at least three visions or goals in your life that have come true. In the middle column, write down what you did to make these three goals a reality. Then, in the final column, write any way you experienced a helping hand from Essence along the way.

Here's an example.

GOAL	WHAT I DID	HELP FROM ESSENCE
Received promotion at work	Took courses that would help me qualify for the job	Browsing online, I saw an ad for a local university. The first page I clicked on showed the class I needed.
	Worked on extra projects to get the attention of my boss	Spouse asked to take a last-minute business trip the same week I worked overtime on the project that brought me to the notice of my boss.
	Kept my eyes and ears open for opportunities Applied in writing for the job	One evening, something told me to leave a message for HR reminding them that I was interested in management. The next morning, they called to say a slot had just opened up. I applied before anyone else.

• • •

Help is always there, whether we're aware of it or not. As Rabbi Abraham Heschel wrote, "God's dream is not to be alone, but to have mankind as a partner in the drama of continuous creation." Essence is your partner in creation, simply waiting for you to draw upon it.

The Five Sources of Power in Connected Manifesting

We each have the power to manifest what we want by focusing on a goal and allowing Essence to help and guide us. For connected manifesting, we must seek alignment with what I call the five sources of power: (1) our connection to Essence, (2) our thoughts and beliefs, (3) our dreams and visions, (4) our intention and desire, (5) our actions and faith. When one or more of these sources are moving in different directions, we experience struggle, obstacles, and detours, even failure. When all five sources of power are aligned, nothing is impossible and our wishes can come true.

THE FIRST SOURCE OF POWER: CONNECTION TO ESSENCE

Unless the Lord builds the house, they labor in vain who build it; Unless the Lord guards the city, the watchmen awaken in vain.

—PSALMS 127:1

I'm sure there have been times that you felt you had accomplished something or acquired something even though you felt the entire universe was against you. But over the years, I've discovered no matter how much you visualize and intend and act, unless you are in alignment with Essence, either your dreams won't come true or achieving them will be an uphill battle—and the end result may or may not be what you want. Connecting with Essence is your best guidance for manifesting the highest and best results. Whenever you want to create something in your life, think of Essence as your best advisor and support, the friend who will tell you the truth about whether this dream will be good for you or not. If the dream is right, Essence will be there to guide and cheer you on and do its best to help you make your dream real. If the dream does not serve your highest good, Essence will be there to help you when you fall or pick up the pieces should the dream harm you in any way.

In general, you can tell if you're on the right track simply by doing an internal check. Does this goal feel right? Are there any internal hitches or hesitations? These kinds of intuitive warnings or sensations may be signs to reassess what you want to manifest. On the other hand, when your goals are in alignment with Essence, you may find yourself experiencing feelings of peace, love, freshness, and a sense that what you are pursuing is true and good and right. Attuning with Essence makes manifestation a pleasure and attaining your goals as easy as breathing.

THE SECOND SOURCE OF POWER: THOUGHTS AND BELIEFS

> When you form a thought within you that's commensurate with Spirit, you form a spiritual prototype that connects you to intention and sets into motion the manifestation of your desires.
>
> —WAYNE W. DYER

Thoughts are powerful. Thoughts are things. They create our reality and can make "a heaven of hell, and a hell of heaven," as

John Milton wrote. I value and respect thoughts because I know their power. Our thoughts shape our actions and determine whether we choose goodness or evil. Science tells us that each day people have approximately fifty thousand thoughts, most of them inconsequential and repetitive: *I'm hungry. I need to call so-and-so. What time is it?* And so on. But the thoughts we choose to focus on can shape our reality. When we focus on positive thoughts of what we want to create, we're tuning our minds to a frequency of Essence that can help us manifest. It's like when you decide to buy a particular model of car. As soon as you purchase the red Volvo, it seems that everywhere you go you see red Volvos! Or perhaps you've had one of those magical days when everything seems to go your way: stoplights turn green, everyone seems to be smiling, and you feel like the luckiest person on earth. Even if you encounter a grumpy person, you say, "They're just having a bad day. I wish they felt as good as I do!" Of course, there are other days when it seems that nothing goes right. Chances are the events of both days weren't all that different; it's just that your thoughts caused you to notice different things. Because thoughts have such power, becoming aware of your thoughts is an essential step in manifesting your goals. Our thoughts are the food of our minds and souls, and in the same way that our health suffers when we eat too much junk food, our mental and spiritual health can suffer when we feed ourselves negative thoughts. That's why it's so important to feed yourself a steady diet of positive thoughts, uplifting information, and inspiring messages. Positive thoughts create positive results. They keep us open to what Essence wants to provide.

The most powerful thoughts are *beliefs*—about ourselves, about the universe, about Essence, and about what is possible and impossible. Beliefs either can create boundaries or free us to dream and achieve. Have you ever said to yourself, "I'd like to have that in my life, but it's just not possible"? Or "It would take too much work or money or time"? Every time you say something along those lines, you're communicating that you're not ready to receive even if Essence is ready to help you create. In the same way you must become aware of your thoughts, you must examine your beliefs so that you can eliminate any possible blockages to the flow of Essence's power.

Negative thoughts will block manifesting your desires. Changing or eliminating negative beliefs can take some work, because they are often based on painful experiences from the past. We also feel that our beliefs cannot be changed because we feel they are "true." But wasn't there something you believed firmly at one time that you know now is completely false? If you ever believed in fairies or Santa Claus, then somewhere along the way you've changed a belief. Perhaps you were told the belief was wrong, or you encountered some kind of evidence that fairies or Santa didn't exist. But in truth, to change your belief, you simply *made a decision* to believe something different. You can do the same with any belief that gets in the way of manifesting. This includes beliefs like, "I'm not good enough," or "It's not possible," or "I don't deserve it," or any other lie you have been telling yourself for years. Essence knows better. Essence sees the truth of who you are—a complete, whole, holy, connected, infinitely capable, and beautiful soul. And once you change your beliefs, you can clear the channel for manifesting more of what you want in your life. Then, as it says in Mark 11:24, "Whatever you ask for in prayer, believe that you have received it, and it will be yours."

THE "ESSENTIAL" BELIEFS ABOUT YOURSELF

Notice any negative beliefs you have about yourself or your abilities. Anytime you find yourself thinking or saying, "I can't," or "I don't deserve it," or "Things don't go my way," and so on, close your eyes and imagine that you are looking at yourself through the eyes of Essence—pure love, goodness, and wisdom. Bring the belief into your mind and ask Essence, "What's the truth?" If the belief is "I can't," the truth may be "God can" or "I can." If the belief is "Things don't go my way," the truth may be "All things are perfect when I'm attuned to Essence." If the belief is "I don't deserve it," the truth may be "I am infinitely deserving because I am love." Anytime the old belief comes up, tell yourself the truth as Essence revealed it.

If you had trouble with this exercise, there may be experiences in your past that you need to handle. I'm a firm believer in using counseling or psychotherapy to handle any challenges from your past that keep you from believing the best about yourself.

When you align your thoughts and beliefs with the highest positive energy, you are better able to draw that energy to you. It's like tuning a radio to a certain frequency: when you tune your thoughts and beliefs to the positive waves Essence is sending, you can connect to its power and use it to shape a better reality in every moment.

THE THIRD SOURCE OF POWER: DREAMS AND VISION

Cherish your vision and your dreams as they are the children of your soul; the blueprints of your ultimate achievements.

—NAPOLEON HILL

Essence is the ultimate creative force in the universe, and all our dreams and visions spring from it. As the Bible says in Proverbs, "Where there is no vision, the people perish." Without dreams and visions to aim for, we are simply stumbling through life from event to event, with no goal, direction, or destination. With dreams and vision, we can walk confidently and purposefully, traveling much further, much faster—as long as our dreams and visions are born from Essence.

Dreams and visions are two different aspects of the same generative force. A dream is a "Wouldn't this be great?" thought or picture. When we dream, we open ourselves to the infinite possibilities of the universe. We don't think of how we're going to create what we dream about; we let our imagination run free. When it comes to manifesting, dreams are often the first step; as poet Carl Sandburg once wrote, "Nothing happens unless first a dream." The wish board I mentioned earlier is a way of capturing your dreams in words and images. To make your dreams realer for you, cut out pictures from magazines, words that represent them, and so on. Post the pictures and words on the board in a form that will attract your eye and uplift your heart.

Our dreams need to possess three qualities. First, they need to *come from deep within our creative impulse,* the place where we are connected to Essence. When we were growing up, some of us had dreams that came from what we thought our parents wanted for us, what we "should" do or who we "should" marry. But inside, we knew they were not our dreams; some other impulse was fighting to express itself. The man whose family always assumed he'd be a doctor felt drawn to become an artist. The woman whose classmates assumed that she would marry right after graduation instead ended up living in Africa, working in a public health clinic. The child of poverty dreamed of building a real estate empire; the child of migrant workers dreamed of going to college. Our dreams are one of our greatest treasures, and we must be true to them even if they are completely alien to our environment and unsupported by the people around us.

Second, we need to *give ourselves permission to dream big.* Essence wants us to be, do, and have great things that will uplift us and help us learn and grow. But far too many of us are afraid to dream big because we think we want or deserve less, or we're afraid of failure and disappointment. I once heard someone equate the universe to an ocean of abundance. The ocean doesn't care whether we bring a teaspoon or a bucket; it's simply there to provide abundance. So why not bring the bucket? Opening yourself to greater abundance and bigger dreams is a service both to yourself and humankind.

Dream lofty dreams, and as you dream,
so shall you become.

—JAMES ALLEN

Third, I believe that *our dreams must be uplifting and empowering, ideally benefiting others as well as ourselves.* Dreams born of Essence are designed to help us grow. A selfish dream that benefits only one person while hurting another carries within it the seeds of destruction. On the other hand, an uplifting and empowering dream that benefits others will have behind it the energy and the blessing of Essence. Even if such a dream fails to happen, there will be lessons and gifts in the attempt.

Once we have a dream, we create a *vision* for how that dream can be made into a reality. Vision makes our dreams concrete. With vision, we add to the emotional pull of our dreams the force of our thoughts and beliefs. Mahatma Gandhi had a dream of a free nation of India, but his vision involved using nonviolence to get the British to leave. While Martin Luther King, Jr., spoke of his dream that "one day the sons of former slaves and the sons of former slave owners will be able to sit down together at the table of brotherhood," his vision included using bus boycotts, protest marches, nonviolent demonstrations, and lunch counter sit-ins. With dreams, you see the destination; with vision, you see the road as well as the destination, the obstacles as well as the goal. Dreams pull you forward by the force of emotion; vision will provide the plan that will keep you going. Dreams bring others to your banner; vision keeps them marching at your side.

You need both dreams and vision to manifest. However, the power of dreams and vision can lead to good or ill. Both Gandhi and Hitler had dreams and visions that inspired them and caused millions to follow them. The poor child who dreams of a real estate empire can become a slumlord or can transform a city by developing blighted areas and providing good jobs and affordable housing. To use the power of your dreams and vision properly, make sure they are connected with Essence. Essence is the touchstone that will ensure that your dreams and vision guide you and others on the highest path.

THE FOURTH SOURCE OF POWER: INTENTION AND DESIRE

Intent is a seed in consciousness, or spirit.
If you pay attention to it, it has within it
the means for its own fulfillment.
—DEEPAK CHOPRA

Our thoughts, beliefs, dreams, and visions combine to create an *intention.* Intention puts the power of the mind behind our dreams and links them to the world and universe. Intention always precedes creation. God first intended that there be light, and then light appeared. In the same way, we must state our intention to Essence so together we may create what we wish to manifest. For your intentions to be powerful, they must be clear and specific. It's not enough to say, "I want to buy a house / get a promotion / find a new relationship / earn more money." What kind of house, and where, and how much will it cost? What job do you want, and by when? Who will be your partner in this new relationship? Instead of asking for a boyfriend or girlfriend, better to ask for a kind person who understands unconditional love, whom you can trust, and who will work as a team for the well-being of you both. Be exact! And remember, your intention should benefit others as well. The clearer your intention and the more people who gain from it, the easier it will be to make it happen.

Intentions also must be reinforced by the power of our *desires.* Desires take us from wishing to doing and keep us going when our will flags. In engaging our desires, however, we must begin by banishing the two great enemies of manifestation: doubt and fear. Doubt afflicts the mind and affects our desires, slowing our progress to our goals. Any doubt or lack of self-worth can stop the creative flow of manifestation in its tracks. The antidote to doubt is certainty. Believe that you can do something and you're more likely to be able to achieve it. As Wayne Dyer said, you must hit the Delete button every time doubt appears.

The second enemy of manifestation, fear, cripples us emotionally and cuts us off from our own resources as well as the presence of Essence. However, fear can be bad or good. Bad fear comes from either a lack of self-worth or a lack of trust both in ourselves and in Essence. Bad fear keeps us small and stops us from attaining the abundance that Essence wants for us. This kind of fear exists to be overcome. To do so takes belief in ourselves and in the ultimate goodness of Essence, and it takes something we'll talk more of later: faith.

Good fear is a result of either common sense or the promptings of our intuition. If your intention is to start your own business but you have little or no training or capital, it's common sense to feel some fear or nervousness. Or if you sit down to sign an offer on a house—the biggest financial commitment of your life so far—it's perfectly natural to feel some fear. The message of fear based on common sense is to *think and prepare.* Make sure you have a sound plan and enough money when you start your business. Before you buy the house, get preapproved for a mortgage with a good rate and reasonable payments—and have a backup plan in case of emergencies. Most good fear will be allayed when we think and prepare.

The other kind of good fear is due to the promptings of our intuition. This kind of fear can arise even when everything seems to be working in our favor. Your intention is to marry your boyfriend or girlfriend, but every time you think about proposing, you feel an irrational discomfort, and later you discover that your partner was cheating on you. Fear can be Essence's warning that this intention is not for our highest good or just won't work out. We need to learn to listen to its promptings, evaluate the circumstances, and take action only when it feels right.

Desire can be a two-edged sword in that it can stop us from listening for the wishes of Essence. At times we say we're asking for guidance, but we're really looking for Essence to validate what we want. "Send me a sign that this is the right person for me," you pray, and then you ignore the lipstick on the collar and the unexplained phone calls. Or you run into that person on the street and think, *That's my sign that he's the one!* and you ignore the street sign next to his head that says, Caution: Rough Road Ahead. Essence is the power behind your intention, but you also have the power to exercise free will and make good or bad choices. You need to be willing to surrender your intention if it's not what will serve you at the highest level.

THE FIFTH SOURCE OF POWER: ACTION AND FAITH

> To accomplish great things we must first dream, then visualize, then plan . . . believe . . . act!
>
> —ALFRED A. MONTAPERT

Once, there was a man who went to church for forty days straight and prayed the same prayer: "Lord, let me win the lottery." On the forty-first day, as he was on his knees, the heavens opened and he heard a divine voice say, "My son, first you have to *buy a ticket.*" You are the agent of Essence when it comes to manifesting your desires. Essence expects us to get out there and do what it takes to create our own dreams. Audrey Hepburn once remarked, "If you ever need a helping hand, you will find them at the end of each of your arms." However, if we put too much focus on our goals without being open to receive, it's like trying to take a gift from someone while our fists are clenched. Great spiritual masters in many traditions talk about the combination of self-effort and grace as being essential to enlightenment, and it's the same with manifestation. You have to put in the effort, but you also have to be open to the collaboration of Essence. As we pursue our goals, we need to pay attention to the subtle or not-so-subtle currents of energy that surround our efforts. Look for coincidences, feelings of being in the flow, small successes, and so on. They will help guide you to reach your goals more quickly.

Also look for any resistance you encounter. Sometimes we feel inner resistance when we come up against our old limitations and ideas of what's possible. In that case, we need to break through the resistance so that we can expand. Attaining goals is like building a muscle; if it's too easy to achieve them, our "manifestation muscle" won't grow. On the other hand, resistance may mean that we're trying to push against the tide of the universe, to accomplish our goals through sheer will rather than in collaboration with Essence. Resistance is always a signal to reconnect with Essence so you may change your approach or redirect your efforts. If you encounter resistance, take a few moments to ask your intuition what your next step should be. Should you persevere or take a break? Focus on this goal or change your direction? You may need to be more flexible in your approach and alert to the different options that Essence is providing you. Listen carefully for these messages and you may find resistance melting away, or you may find yourself with increased resolve to push through and become stronger.

When it comes to connected manifesting, there is a paradox: we must pursue our goals while being unattached to the results. We must say to Essence, "I will do everything I can, but I recognize that the ultimate result is up to you." Deepak Chopra describes it as acting without expectations but with an intended outcome. He writes, "An intended outcome without expectations or attachment orchestrates its own fulfillment." If you wish to see the paradox of action and nonattachment, watch the competitors at the Special Olympics. The motto of the Special Olympics is, "Let me win, but if I cannot win, let me be brave in the attempt." These young athletes, who all have intellectual disabilities, compete with every fiber of their being and celebrate when they finish, whether they are the first or the last. They understand that greatness lies not in the result but in the attempt and in who they become as they pursue their goals. When you pursue your aims while being unattached to the results, you feel enormous freedom and joy. You can celebrate the results that Essence has created through you and for you, knowing that the greatest accomplishment lies in who you have become. Ultimately, we must have faith that Essence is with us, and whatever happens in the course of our path to manifestation was meant for our greatest good. With faith, we can put the power of our emotions and will, our desires and intention behind the creation of our dreams and visions. Desire is the fuel, intention is the vehicle, vision is the road, and faith is the centerline that guides us and helps us take our dreams from potential to reality.

Manifesting in Alignment with Essence

Tuning in to Essence to manifest something in your life can be as simple as asking. Here's a version of the process you learned in chapter 3.

STEP 1: CREATE A CLEAR FOCUS FOR YOUR REQUEST AND PREPARE TO TUNE IN.

Start by writing your intention. Next to it, write the reasons you wish to manifest this goal. Check for any negative beliefs or energies around your intention and clear them out before you make your request of Essence. If there are any negative thoughts influencing you, turn them to positive thoughts. Once you have your intention, go to the space where you meditate, or find a quiet corner with no distractions. Keep pen and paper handy to jot down any messages you receive. Always surround yourself with white light and say a prayer that any communication comes only from the highest and best energy of Essence.

STEP 2: BRING YOUR INTENTION INTO YOUR MIND AND HEART AND LISTEN FOR WHAT ESSENCE WISHES FOR YOU.

Take a few deep breaths, clear your mind, and turn your focus to the present moment. Let yourself settle into a connected, relaxed, and balanced state. Now, think of your intention. Hold it in your mind for a few moments, and then place it in your heart. Allow any feelings about your intention to blossom. If it is truly a "heart's desire," something that will benefit you and others, you'll feel peaceful, centered, and aligned. Make note of any thoughts, feelings, or impressions. If any doubts or fears arise, ask Essence to tell you where they are coming from and ask for help in clearing them out. Ask, "Do you want me to have this in my life, or do you have other plans?" You may need to modify your intention or put it aside for a while, or change it altogether. You must believe that Essence wants only what is best for you, even when that is contrary to your intention. Trust that whatever you receive or do not receive will be for your highest good and greatest growth.

STEP 3: RELEASE YOUR INTENTION AND, WITH FAITH IN ESSENCE'S GUIDANCE, TAKE ACTION TO MANIFEST YOUR INTENTION.

Intentions are waiting for our hands to make them real in collaboration with Essence. We need to take action, and at the same time give Essence a chance to help. As Goethe wrote, "Destiny grants us our wishes, but in its own way, in order to give us something beyond our wishes." You also must have patience. Things will come into your life on God's time, not yours. Be patient, stay alert, and trust. Be flexible and attuned to the desires of Essence as well as your own.

Karma and Destiny

As we are, so we do; and as we do, so is it done to us; we are the builders of our fortunes.

—RALPH WALDO EMERSON

Two other factors affect our ability to manifest: karma and destiny. Each lifetime is like one chapter of a very long novel, where characters recur and the events of previous chapters affect what happens in this one. In many of my readings, I can sense the karmic interconnections that link us to people here on Earth and spirits on the other side. Remember the family who had lost their mother, Susanna, ten years earlier? The father had recently gotten into a new relationship, even though he still mourned for his deceased wife. I told him, "The woman you're in a relationship with now?

Susanna owed karma to her from other lifetimes. Before they came to Earth, they made a pact that Susanna would marry you first and then this other woman would marry you. Susanna is very happy that you're together now."

The karma we have created in our past lifetimes can help or hurt us. The good and the evil we do has an impact on our souls and on our lifetimes here on Earth. If you were greedy in your last lifetime, you may be born into poverty in this one. If you helped a lot of people or were unselfish in your last lifetime, this time you might have an easy life with good relationships. That's not to say that you should use karma as a cop-out for not trying your best, or for failing to call on Essence to help you manifest. The only way we can keep progressing is to make the most of the karma we bring with us, and to do our best to create good karma this time around.

If karma is a result of what we did in previous lifetimes, destiny is what we are slated to experience in this one. Our destiny includes the lessons we are supposed to learn, the people we're supposed to meet, and the events that we are supposed to experience. Some elements of our destiny are fixed, but most are not. Our past karma helps *shape* our destiny but does not determine it completely. Think of karma as the set of cards you have dealt yourself. Will the cards have an impact on your life? Of course. But there are an infinite number of ways you can play the same set of cards. Destiny is the outcome of the game.

I read for a family whose father, Andre—a famous singer—had passed away. Andre had a message for his teenage son. "You want to be an actor now, but your dad is saying that one day you'll want to work behind the scenes in business, as a manager, and you'll be really good at it," I told the boy. "He says you're a 'silent giant' because you're powerful and strong, and he's proud you bear his name." I could see how happy young Andre was to hear the encouraging words from his father's spirit. This young man's destiny was pointing him toward a career in business—but his life will be shaped by the choices he makes along the way.

In another case, a woman, Maria, who had lost her depressed husband to suicide, came to me for a reading. (Suicide is *never* the answer to bad karma. Suicide is always a choice, not a destiny—and a very bad choice in the long run. Not only does it devastate the people who are left behind, but it also cuts us off from the lessons we're supposed to learn in this lifetime. When people cut their lives short, they still have to learn the lessons they missed. We can't skip lessons; we simply come back and learn them with even more complicated karma from the suicide.) I immediately picked up that her husband was with his grandmother on the other side. Maria looked so sad as she told me that the hardest thing for her was that the love of his family wasn't strong enough to save her husband, Dennis. "Everyone thought they could fix him, but he didn't want to fix himself," I told her. "He didn't leave a note, did he? I feel that he was tempting fate by jumping on the tracks to see if he could make it past before the train came. If he'd planned this, he would have left a note, and he says he is truly sorry." Then I picked up on something else that surprised her. "Dennis says there's someone new coming into your life. You have a karmic connection with this new man. So even though Dennis wasn't wise about making choices for himself, you need to make the right choices about this new relationship for yourself and your son."

What we do with what we are given will determine our destiny and the progress of our soul from lifetime to lifetime. Whether the events of our lives are predestined, a result of past karma, or something we are encountering for the first time, our choices create our destiny both here and in the hereafter. That's why it is so important to stay in touch with Essence when it comes to choosing what we wish to manifest. Of course, getting in touch with Essence doesn't keep you from making mistakes. Mistakes are a part of our process and our progress. Perhaps you got into a relationship that you realized was a mistake, but you grew so much that you were ready for the love of your life. And, as I said earlier, certain things are predestined for us to experience, whether they are mistakes, painful choices, or a life of ease. But for the 90 percent of life choices that are not predestined, Essence can help us choose what will be for our highest good. And the highest good should always be the goal for anything we wish to manifest in our lives.

YOUR SOUL'S ENERGY BOOSTERS

- Manifesting turns dreams into realities.
- Adopt the belief that "God doesn't make junk." You are a part of Essence, and as such, you deserve to see yourself as beautiful and whole.
- In manifesting, we tap into the power of Essence to bring the unseen into physical form. You, too, can make a wish board.
- Life is a school and our primary purpose on Earth is to learn the lessons that will give us the greatest growth.
- We must trust that Essence always knows what's for our greatest benefit.
- We are part of an interconnected web of energy, and our goals, intentions, and desires intersect with the goals, intentions, and desires of others.

- Thoughts are powerful. Thoughts are things. They create our reality and can make "a heaven a hell, and a hell of heaven."
- Positive thoughts create positive results. Attitude is everything.
- Changing or eliminating negative beliefs can take some work because they are often based on negative experiences from the past.
- Fear cripples us emotionally and cuts us off from our own resources as well as the presence of Essence.
- Good fear is a result of either common sense or the promptings of our intuition.
- Desire is the fuel, intention is the vehicle, vision is the road, and faith is the centerline that guides us and helps us take our dreams from potential to reality.
- Two factors affect our ability to manifest: karma and destiny.

FIVE

Today Is Your Best Day!

Today a new sun rises for me; everything lives, everything is animated, everything seems to speak to me of my passion, everything invites me to cherish it.

—NINON DE LENCLOS

Imagine you wake up on the morning of what you know will be a truly special day. Maybe it's your birthday, or the birthday of a loved one; maybe someone dear to you is coming to see you after a long absence. Maybe it's the day you start your dream job or leave it for a well-deserved retirement. Maybe it's your child's graduation, or their first day of school. On such mornings, you are filled with excited anticipation and a tingling happiness. You look forward to every moment of the day ahead. What if you had that feeling every single morning? Because here's the truth: *every day has the potential to be the best day of your life.* In the busyness of life, it's all too easy to forget what a precious gift each day is. Even when we're beset with what can seem like insurmountable barriers to happiness, Essence has given us yet another day in which to find peace and contentment. Every day is a blank slate, and you have a chance to make the day the way you want it. Even if your past weighs you down and your future seems clouded, in truth all you have is today, and in that day all things are possible. As an old Inuit proverb says, "Yesterday is ashes, tomorrow wood. Only today does the fire burn brightly."

We find our closest connection to Essence when we cherish the day we have been given. Think of the times in your life when you have been the happiest—the kiss you always remember, your child's first smile or first step, crossing the finish line of a race, the glimpse of a distant mountain or ocean that took your breath away, sitting by the fire with your loved one in your arms, running with your dog on a beach, and so on. In that moment, you were fully present and connected to Essence. These moments may be dramatic or prosaic, a lifetime highlight or a simple bit of grace, but they are far from ordinary. Indeed, they are the truest experience of life. And we can have such moments at almost any time if we but turn our attention to the gift of the present.

Like most people, I can miss out on the present because I am planning for the future. I forget to acknowledge and appreciate the gift of each day. As we learned in the last chapter, the future does merit consideration when it comes to manifesting our desires, but when we lose the present in our focus on the future, we are throwing away a gift that will never come again. I have seen this frequently with people who come for readings because they failed to say something to a loved one, to heal a breach or do something kind, and then they lost that person to death. Such regrets weigh heavy on our hearts and on the spirits of those who have passed over. That's why it's so important not to live *for* today necessarily but to live *in* today.

There is an ancient Sanskrit prayer called "Salutation to the Dawn":

Look to this day!
For it is life, the very life of life.
In its brief course lie all the verities
and realities of your existence:
the bliss of growth,
the glory of action,
the splendor of beauty.
For yesterday is but a dream,
and tomorrow is only a vision;
but today, well lived, makes every yesterday
a dream of happiness
and every tomorrow a vision of hope.

To make the most of your life, live as if today were your last day on earth, or the last day of the people you love. Live as if each moment were precious, because it is. When you live with this consciousness, every day can indeed be the best day of your life.

Start Your Day with an Inner Attitude Check

If God adds another day to our life,
let us receive it gladly.

—SENECA THE YOUNGER

"Well begun is half-done," I used to hear when I was growing up, or "She got out of the wrong side of the bed" if someone was grumpy.

The way we start our day can affect our ability to receive the day's goodness. I suggest that, whenever possible, you start every morning with a few quiet moments of prayer or reflection or simply saying thank you. The great poet Kahlil Gibran wrote, "Wake at dawn with a winged heart and give thanks for another day of loving." We have been given a beautiful gift in a new day, and we can choose to start it with gratitude and contentment, connected with our inner source of love. Sit quietly, write down any messages that may come up, and then apply them as you go through your daily routine. Connecting with Essence through prayer and gratitude is especially valuable in times of stress or unhappiness, because that is when we need its support and strength. Viktor Frankl, psychologist, Holocaust survivor, and author of *Man's Search for Meaning,* wrote that in the concentration camps when a man could no longer endure the horrific realities of every day, he often would find solace in his spiritual life, which even the Nazis could not destroy. If we are facing a day that we know will be challenging, the best thing we can do is to call upon Essence in the morning. As it says in Psalm 27, "The Lord is the strength of my life; of whom shall I be afraid?"

Once you have connected with Essence, check your inner attitude. Are you in a good mood or a bad mood? If something's bothering you, what is it? Did you get a good night's sleep? Your physical condition can affect your attitude. Are you worried about facing something today? Call upon Essence to show you what to do. Is it something that's a residue from the past? Leave the past in the past and welcome the present. Is it something that you might face in the future? Resolve to "do what you can, with what you have, where you are," as Theodore Roosevelt wrote. The attitude with which you face the day will make it your best day or your worst. Checking your inner attitude should be something you do when you wake up. Just like flossing your teeth, it will help you stay healthy and keep smiling.

Even if you awake with a bad attitude or just feeling lousy, don't take your bad feelings out on other people; all it does is spread your pain around. If you find yourself in a bad mood, resolve to treat others even better than you would if you were in a good mood. Give someone your seat on the train. If a guy is trying to cut in front of you on the road, give him a smile instead of the finger. Your attitude will improve every time you choose to do something kind, and you may never know what your kindness may mean to someone else.

EASY ATTITUDE ADJUSTMENTS

An easy way to change your attitude in the morning is to think of something that makes you happy. What do you like to do more than anything in the world? Who's your favorite person? What's the best memory of your life? What's your favorite place to relax? Put yourself back into those memories. Thinking of these things will shift your focus to better times and will help you shift your attitude. You also can imagine yourself surrounded by bright white light or sunlight. Let the energy of the light fill you up and protect you from any negative feelings or occurrences. Take yourself in that bright white light and put yourself in a mirrored egg. Use the mirror to bounce off anything negative that may come near you. Then say, "Anything that is in, near, around, or about me that is not of light, go back to where you came from."

Another great remedy for a bad mood or attitude is to get out into nature. There's nothing more healing than the natural beauty of this world, but most of us are becoming more and more cut off from this important source of energy. When I feel tired or burned out, being in nature gives me a sense of balance along with greater calm and peace. Anne Frank wrote, "The best remedy for those who are afraid, lonely or unhappy is to go outside, somewhere where they can be quiet, alone with the heavens, nature and God. Because only then does one feel that all is as it should be and that God wishes to see people happy, amidst the simple beauty of nature. As long as this exists, and it certainly always will, I know that then there will always be comfort for every sorrow, whatever the circumstances may be. And I firmly believe that nature brings solace in all troubles." Even though Anne Frank was in hiding from the Nazis and didn't go outside for two years, she understood how nature can help us connect with Essence. Make it a part of your daily routine to be outside. Take a walk or ride a bicycle in a park or by the water. Go on a hike in the forest or the mountains. Get your hands dirty in a garden. Sit on a park bench and feed the birds. Take a child or a pet for a walk and watch how they connect with the world around them. Exercise and walking in nature can clear your mind and help your energy. If something is bothering you, write on a wide leaf the thought or circumstance that is causing you trouble, take it outside on a windy day, and let the wind carry it away. Let the thought go and have faith that Essence will give you everything you need to handle whatever comes up in your life.

Dr. Heartsill Wilson once wrote a poem about the importance of each day.

This is the beginning of a new day.
I have been given this day to use as I will.
I can waste it, or use it.

I can make it a day long to be remembered for its joy, its beauty and its achievements, or it can be filled with pettiness.
What I do today is important because I am exchanging a day of my life for it.
When tomorrow comes this day will be gone forever, but I shall hold something which I have traded for it.
It may be no more than a memory, but if it is a worthy one I shall not regret the price.

Remember, today is a gift that will never come again. Therefore, start your day well, and spend it as wisely as you can.

Walking in Partnership with Essence

To those leaning on the sustaining infinite,
today is big with blessings.

—MARY BAKER EDDY

In the same way that you should endeavor to start each morning with a positive attitude, you should do your best to walk with Essence throughout your day. Remember the law of attraction: what you focus on creating inside yourself, you will notice or attract more of in the outside world. Therefore, approach your day with a positive outlook and an expectation that Essence will be your partner as it unfolds. When we're aware, we can see miracles surrounding us—so-called magic moments, instances when time seems to stop and our hearts leap. A special look in a loved one's eyes. A flower just bursting into bloom. The laugh of a child. A magnificent rainbow. A sunset in a stormy sky. These are times when our whole being stops and marvels at the wonder of life. We treasure such moments for their magic, and also because we know they are ephemeral. We cannot hold on to them, try as we might. But we *can* hold them in memory and use them to connect to Essence at any time. Moments like this are unexpected gifts from the universe, and I believe we can find such moments every day if we only look for them.

Maintaining a connection with Essence should be an ongoing focus within your day. This isn't complicated, thank goodness; it simply requires that you remember Essence every now and then and check in using your intuition. It's like having one of those mobile phones with a radio or "push to talk" feature. At the touch of a button, you can call the person who has a phone on the same frequency (at least, that's how I think it works—I'm a technological Mr. Magoo or rather Ms. Magoo). Your intuition can help you create the same kind of "push to talk" connection with Essence. Throughout your day, every now and then take a moment for an intuitive "connection check." Focus inside and say, "I'm here, Essence—anything you want me to know?" Simply checking in will help you lead your day more closely in tune with Essence's guidance.

This inner connection serves us particularly well when things aren't going smoothly. In such moments, asking for help and direction can get us through. Remember, we're here to learn lessons and to grow, and if everything went smoothly, we would do neither. So don't expect your life to be completely happy or for there to be no tough times. When you keep a strong "link" to Essence, however, you *can* expect to be given the support to deal with whatever occurs. There's a familiar story about a woman who dies and goes to heaven. She looks back on her life and sees it as a walk along a beautiful beach. She can see her footprints in the sand, and alongside them are another set of prints—God's. But she notices that during the toughest times of her life, there was only one set of prints. "How could you desert me in my times of greatest need?" she cries to God.

"I didn't," God answers. "Those were the times when I was carrying you."

One of the best ways to keep in touch with Essence throughout the day is to focus completely on the task at hand (distractions can sometimes be trickster energies taking you away from accomplishing your goal). Most of us go through our days and do our allotted tasks with some energy, enthusiasm, and focus but not with all our minds and hearts. Those who are enlightened realize that every action, all our work, when done with complete attention and love, becomes an expression of Essence manifesting in the world. Work then becomes an offering. It also is a pleasure. Have you ever been so focused on what you were doing that you lost track of time? In those moments, you were connected to the timeless nature of Essence. You were completely in the present moment, absorbed in your task and fulfilled by its execution. You can create those occasions at will, simply by putting your focus completely on your work and doing it with love. "Your daily life is your temple and your religion," wrote Kahlil Gibran. Any kind of activity, from routine physical labor to caring for children to the most complicated intellectual endeavor, can be sacred when it is done with pure focus and selfless love. That doesn't mean that you don't gain from your work; in fact, I believe you will gain more when you put both your focus and love into it. It does mean that you find a purpose for your work that goes beyond duty or obligation or personal gain. When you consciously choose to make Essence your partner in your daily work, you will find your work will become more joyful and fulfilling.

As we walk through our days, Essence asks us to look for the best in ourselves and others. Looking for the best doesn't mean seeing everything through rose-colored glasses. Certainly there are bad things in the world, and people who may not wish us well or who see our efforts and needs as competing with theirs. Essence made us to look for the highest, and Essence also made a natural world where big animals eat little animals and survival is the primary drive. But here's the difference: when we have evolved to the point where we are born as human beings, we have been given the gift of a spirit and soul with a drive to evolve and grow into something that ever more closely resembles the Essence from which we come. When we decide to look for the best in ourselves and others, we don't ignore the energies and people that may hold us down, but we do hold them and ourselves to a higher standard of behavior. Say someone at work decides to let a shoddy job go through because it would be too much effort to fix it. "The boss won't know that it's not up to par," your coworker says. "Why spend the time to make it right when it won't make any difference?" But it will make a difference—perhaps not to the product but to the standards the group holds for itself. It will take courage for you to say, "We need to fix this because we don't do shoddy work," but when you are walking through your day with Essence, you will know when speaking up is the right thing to do. And when we do our best, Essence will provide for us the support we need. The great scientist and writer Booker T. Washington wrote, "Any man's life will be filled with constant and unexpected encouragement if he makes up his mind to do his level best each day." No matter what people's standards are around you, make a decision today to do your best, and watch the universe applaud.

Looking for the best always begins in ourselves. We have to

make the decision to return good for evil, to turn the other cheek, and to step out of the "eye for an eye" mind-set that creates so much conflict in the world. Imagine that one morning you get into an argument with your spouse. Things start to escalate and you both leave the house angry. Usually during the day you call or text each other a couple of times, but today neither of you picks up the phone. When you get home after work, you're greeted by a frosty silence. Even if you believe you were in the right, if you look for the best in yourself, you will choose to be the first to apologize. You say, "I'm sorry that I didn't call you today. I love you too much to be mad at you. Can we talk this out? I want to understand your side of things." Our best selves are conscious, caring, seeking to understand rather than be understood. It's easier to help others when we stay connected with the balance and peace of Essence. We can come up with the simple words and actions that can make the biggest difference. Not too long ago, I heard of a woman who decided that for an entire day she would be kind to everyone she met. She actively looked for chances to smile at people, to lend them a hand, and to put their needs before hers. After work she went to the grocery store. As she stood in line with a full cart, she noticed that right behind her was a frazzled-looking young mother holding a few items in one arm and a crying toddler in the other.

The first woman smiled and said, "Please go ahead of me." The young mother smiled in relief, said, "Thank you!" and put her items on the counter. After her transaction was completed, she turned to the first woman and said, "We've lived in this community for only a couple of months, and it's been really tough. Today I said to myself, 'Unless someone does something kind today, I'm going to move back to my old town.' Your letting me go in front of you was a sign that things are going to work out. Thank you so much!" When we partner with Essence in being kind, in paying attention to others, and in consciously choosing to be our best, we not only experience miracles, we become an active partner in their creation.

> **You have the capacity to change the world within a moment. All you must do is make a simple choice. Are you going to choose a world of love and gratitude, or a tortured world filled with discontent and impoverishment?**
>
> —MASARU EMOTO, *THE HIDDEN MESSAGES OF WATER*

Along with focusing completely on work and noticing magic moments, I'm a big believer in actively creating a day that you can be proud of and love. Many of us vacillate between simply letting our days unfold without a plan and having them so completely and totally planned out that there's no room for spontaneity. Plans can be valuable; they help us get things done. However, I suggest that you approach your day with a plan that includes space for reflection, recreation, and the unexpected. Make it a priority to have at least one moment of happiness, fun, joy, or peace each day. That may mean a dance class or workout at lunch, a walk on the beach, or reading or listening to something inspiring, or just putting your feet up and resting for fifteen minutes. As a Sanskrit proverb says, "He who allows his day to pass by without practicing generosity and enjoying life's pleasures is like a blacksmith's bellows: he breathes, but does not live."

I believe we create our days by the choices we make in every moment. We can choose to shelter our heart from fear or to act in such a way that we give off light and love, and thus attract it to ourselves. We can choose to be hurtful or helpful. We can choose to be cowardly or courageous. We can choose to do what's easy, or to do what's right. We can choose to focus on our own needs first, or include others in our efforts. We can choose to blunder ahead and do things the hard way, or to listen to and be guided by Essence. By our choices, we create the world around us. The best way to walk through your day is to keep your focus on your goals while continuing to be open to Essence's gifts.

But what about the things that come into our lives that no one would ever want? In the same way that there is both dark and light in the universe, pain and trouble are a part of all lives, whether we choose them or not. But we *always* have a choice to look for the ways that our pain and problems can benefit us. The deal that falls through teaches you how to talk to the next client. The lover that cheats on you makes you stand up for yourself and say, "No more." A disease or disability or accident causes you to have to receive for the first time in your life, and you learn how many people truly love you. I once read for a young lady, Yolanda, whose mother had been ill with terminal cancer and wanted to die at home. Yolanda was tending to her mom in her mother's house. One day, she brought to the house an item that needed to be repaired, but she had forgotten that her mother was horribly allergic to glue. Mom had a bad reaction to the fumes; they rushed her to the hospital, but she died. Yolanda felt she had caused her mother's death. But when her mother spoke through me, she had a very different message for her daughter. "If your mom hadn't died from the allergic reaction, she would have had a much longer, drawn-out death from cancer. She would have suffered a great deal. She says that this was a blessing in disguise," I told Yolanda. She had never considered this view because she wanted to keep her mother with her as long as possible. But Essence was more compassionate and caring. The "accident" cut short the suffering of the mother, and the reading Yolanda received allowed her to be at peace.

As Saint Basil wrote, "Many a man curses the rain that falls upon his head, and knows not that it brings abundance to drive away hunger." We have the choice to look at our problems from a different perspective and to search actively for a meaning that keeps us connected to Essence. Even if we can't see it in the moment, we can always have faith that what happens in our lives is for our greatest good.

The Messages Around Us

Let your hook always be cast. In the stream where you least expect it, there will be fish.

—OVID

If you are truly in tune with Essence during your day, you'll find that you often receive messages to guide you. Sometimes these messages are subtle inner energy shifts. At other times, there will be moments where you make a connection between what is happening and what Essence wants you to know or how it wants you to act. Our responsibility is to "pay careful attention to God's whispers," as music producer Quincy Jones once said. For some people, there are particular signs that appear when Essence wants to communicate with them. A client of mine will be walking down the street of the busy city where she lives, thinking about a decision she has to make or a person she's about to meet, and she'll come across a feather lying on the sidewalk. Based on past experience, she knows that feathers are a signal that she's on the right track. Objects like feathers that appear more often than can be explained by coincidence or happenstance may be a sign particular to you. Pay attention to these occurrences and see if they are connected to situations where you need guidance, help, or advice.

For example, you're wondering about whether you should leave your current job and look for another. You've heard some rumors about the company being in trouble, but nothing definite. As you walk down the street on your lunch hour, your eyes are drawn to a sign in a store window: GOING OUT OF BUSINESS SALE! Or perhaps you sit down on a park bench to eat your lunch, and a section of newspaper blows against your leg. It's a page from today's Help Wanted ads. In both cases, you feel a little shiver or flash of intuition. You start looking for a new job immediately. A month after you start at your new company, the old one announces that it's filing for bankruptcy.

Every day, we can receive messages from Essence, if we are open to them. This includes messages from people who have passed over. Our loved ones in spirit use many simple, natural ways to let us know they are still with us. Some people see doves or hummingbirds more frequently or in new places after the death of a loved one. Others will notice things like shiny dimes that appear in strange places. Not too long ago, I saw a yellow bird, dead, on the side of the road. While I never predict death in my readings, Yellow Feather was my mom's spirit guide, and I said to a friend of mine, "That's a sign from my mom to prepare me; I think someone I know is going to pass over." The same day, I heard that the husband of another friend had died. One little boy told me that not long after his mother had passed away, a bird had come into the house for three days straight. It hadn't panicked, as most birds would; instead, it had flown around and took its time leaving. "Was that my mother?" the boy asked.

"It was a sign from your mom that she's in heaven with your grandma," I told him.

Another gentleman reported that every time he went to visit his wife's grave, there was a white butterfly either flying around or perched on the top of her tombstone. He wanted to know if that was a sign. "Yes, especially if you felt it was from her," I answered. "Butterflies are an especially good sign, as they represent evolution to a higher state. Seeing a butterfly means your wife is free."

We ignore the inner promptings of intuition and other messages from Essence at our peril. Take the time to fine-tune your interactions with the world. Use your sixth sense to keep pointed in the right direction so you can avoid potential obstacles and reap the greatest benefit from your day. Pastor Maltbie D. Babcock wrote, "Be on the lookout for mercies. The more we look for them, the more of them we will see." Essence offers us its mercies through our intuitive tuning in to the events of our daily life. It's up to us to accept its loving protection and guidance.

Dealing with Life's Opportunities and Obstacles

Everyone has bad breaks, but everyone also has opportunities. The man who can smile at his breaks and grab his chances gets on.

—SAMUEL GOLDWYN

There's a story called "Acres of Diamonds" that is based on a true incident involving a farmer in Africa. One evening, a wandering holy man knocked at the farmhouse door and asked for shelter. The farmer invited the man in, fed him a good meal, and sat up with him as the holy man talked of his travels. The farmer was fascinated by one tale in particular of a precious stone the holy man called a *diamond.* "The most valuable thing in the world, and the most beautiful," the holy man said. "They are very rare, but you can find them if you look hard enough. Just one diamond can make a man rich."

After the holy man left the next day, the farmer couldn't get the diamond out of his mind. Within the week, he left his prosperous farm to search for diamonds. For many years, he traveled the world. He spent all his money and then some in his quest. He was forced to sell his farm to keep searching. Finally, broke, emaciated, despondent, and far from home, he threw himself into the ocean and drowned.

Years later, the holy man came back to the part of Africa where the farmer had lived. Again he asked for shelter, and the man who had bought the farm welcomed him and told him to sit by the fire while he made them both a meal. The holy man looked at an object on the mantel and exclaimed, "The farmer found his diamond! It's the biggest one I've ever seen!"

"Oh, that's just a rock I picked up in the stream and brought home because it was pretty," said the new owner of the farm.

"My son, that's a diamond," the holy man insisted. "Show me where you found it." The new owner took the holy man to the stream. There were literally dozens of diamonds in the streambed. The property was located on one of the richest diamond mines in Africa. Neither the old farmer nor the new was aware of the wealth they possessed.

Essence offers us an abundance of opportunities in the course of each day. Opportunities for success, kindness, happiness, enjoyment, peace, connection, love, growth . . . and far too often we walk by these opportunities because we simply don't see them as such, or we're caught up in the story inside our heads. We're like the farmer who never bothered to see the riches in his own backyard. We see the old woman with too many parcels and we don't see the opportunity to lend a helping hand. We see the wind rustling through the leaves in the park and we don't see the opportunity to take a moment to breathe and appreciate nature. We receive a phone call from a loved one and don't see it as an opportunity to connect and care, an opportunity that may never come again. We overhear a coworker asking for help on a project and miss the opportunity to volunteer and perhaps add to our skills and create a better team at work. Congregationalist pastor Albert E. Dunning once wrote, "Great opportunities come to all, but many do not know they have met them. The only preparation to take advantage of them is simple fidelity to watch what each day brings." Every day is rich with opportunity; every moment is a chance to notice and act, if we just follow our own inner voice.

Blessings in our lives can take the form of both opportunities and challenges, but we rarely see our challenges and obstacles for the opportunities that they truly are. Essence brings obstacles into our day so we may continue to grow, not just by how we handle the obstacles outside but also by how we hold the obstacles inside. As Deepak Chopra says, "Difficult situations don't create suffering; resistance to *what is* creates suffering." Whenever we resist the circumstances in our lives, we create suffering. Think of the obstacles that you have encountered. When have they caused you the most pain? Usually when you have fought against the obstacle or resisted it. If you have ever said to yourself, "That's not fair!" or "No one should have to go through this," you have felt inner resistance.

Try this experiment. The next time you feel physical pain, notice your reaction to it. Can you feel your inner resistance? Can you feel tension in your body? Are you saying, "I shouldn't have this pain!"? Before taking a painkiller, try simply acknowledging and accepting the pain. If it's a headache, say to yourself, "I accept the fact that my head hurts." Many people notice an immediate decrease of tension and resistance in the body. The pain may not disappear, but frequently it diminishes simply because they have accepted the fact of its existence. The same can be done with the obstacles you may face in life. Take a moment to connect to Essence and say, "I accept this obstacle, this problem. You have given this to me for a reason. Help me understand and make the best of this circumstance." When you release your resistance and accept your circumstances, you open yourself to help from Essence. In *A New Earth*, Eckhart Tolle writes: "Whatever action you take in a state of inner resistance . . . will create more outer resistance, and the universe will not be on your side; life will not be helpful. When you yield internally, when you surrender, a new dimension of consciousness opens up. . . . If action is possible or necessary, your action will be in alignment with the whole and supported by creative intelligence. . . . Circumstances and people then become helpful, cooperative. If no action is possible, you rest in the peace and inner stillness that come with surrender. You rest in God."

On the other hand, have you encountered obstacles that you regarded as something you simply needed to overcome or go around? Maybe you asked someone out on a date and they turned you down, but you kept asking until they said yes. Or you had a problem to solve at the office and the first three solutions didn't work—but the fourth solution did, and actually solved two other problems at the same time. Randy Pausch, a remarkable professor whom you'll meet later, once said, "The brick walls are not there to keep us out. The brick walls are there to give us a chance to show how badly we want something."

Being connected to Essence may not change your life's circumstances, but it can change your experience of those life circumstances. As someone once said, "Pain is inevitable, but *suffering* is optional." An inspirational example of this is the physicist Stephen Hawking. He was diagnosed with amyotrophic lateral sclerosis (ALS) in 1963 when he was only twenty-one years old. He was told that his life expectancy was around three years and that he would die a long, slow, lingering death as he lost all control of his body. When Dr. Hawking received the diagnosis, he described himself as bored with life and depressed. But then he had a couple of dreams, one where he was going to be executed, and another where he sacrificed his life to save other people. He writes that these dreams made him realize that his life was worth living and that he could do a lot of good with the time he had, no matter how long or short. In the fifty-five years since his diagnosis, Dr. Hawking has been recognized as one of the top theoretical physicists of our age. He coauthored dozens of scientific papers, and his book *A Brief History of Time* was a number-one bestseller. Over those same fifty-five years, Dr. Hawking also became a quadriplegic, unable to speak or move without assistance. Dr. Hawking experienced more of what most of us would consider "pain" than any human being should have to bear, yet he described himself as "lucky" because his disease progressed so slowly and the support of family and colleagues had allowed him to accomplish his dreams. His life experience had been dictated not by his circumstances but what he had chosen to do with what he had been given. Dr. Hawking crossed over in 2018 at the age of seventy-six.

No matter what happens in the course of a day, we have the opportunity to make it the best day of our lives by connecting with Essence and deciding to view whatever comes our way as gifts from the universe. When we do so, opportunities and obstacles become two sides of the same coin. Our suffering disappears and we can feel joy and peace. We can go through our day loving and being loved, pursuing goals while unattached to their attainment, learning and growing and becoming ever more of our best, truest nature.

End Your Day with Reflection and Gratitude

Happy the man, and happy he alone
He who can call today his own
He who, secure within, can say
"Tomorrow, do thy worst
For I have lived today."

—JOHN DRYDEN

In 2007, a video posted on the internet was viewed by more than ten million people. Called "The Last Lecture," it was a speech given by Randy Pausch, Ph.D., a professor at Carnegie Mellon University in the United States. Dr. Pausch had pancreatic cancer, and his doctors told him he had three to six months to live. But to watch the lecture, you would never know he was ill. He was upbeat, even joyful, finding the humor in everything, including his situation. He did one-armed push-ups and declared, "Unless you can come up here and do the same, you're not allowed to pity me." His speech, entitled "Really Achieving Your Childhood Dreams," talked about the value of attitude and optimism, overcoming barriers and obstacles, and the all-encompassing importance of love and family. Randy Pausch died in July 2008, ten months after his last lecture, surrounded by his family and friends. His story has inspired millions all over the world.

What is life? It is the flash of a firefly in the night.
It is the breath of a buffalo in the wintertime.
It is the little shadow which runs across the grass
And loses itself in the sunset.

—CROWFOOT, NATIVE AMERICAN ORATOR

Ultimately, all of us walk the same path as Randy Pausch. We may not see the end approaching so quickly, nor know what will be the cause of our demise. But our days on this earth will come to an end, probably far faster than we think. Every day, we have the opportunity to decide what we wish to trade our time for—whether we will make even the most ordinary of days valuable because of our attitude and contributions, or cast aside our time like the unnoticed diamonds that lay under the farmer's feet. And every evening we have the opportunity to reflect on the events of our day, to evaluate our actions and hesitations, to see where we have succeeded and where we have failed, to appreciate the love we have given and received and to mourn the opportunities for love that we have missed. We can commit ourselves anew to walk ever more closely with Essence as our friend and guide, to trust that we will be given what we need to handle what comes into our lives, and to take the actions needed to learn and grow.

Once we have reflected on our day, we need to let it go so we may awake tomorrow with a clean slate. As Deepak Chopra writes,

"Before you go to sleep at night, witness the whole day and tell yourself, *It's already a dream. It's gone.*" At the end of the day, if we offer everything to Essence—good, bad, pleasant, unpleasant, failures, and successes—we are only giving back to Essence what it has given to us. We are trusting Essence to take care of us and those we love as well as our treasures. Releasing our day to God will mean a clean slate and a light heart when we wake tomorrow.

God gave you a gift of 86,400 seconds today.
Have you used one to say, "Thank you"?
—WILLIAM ARTHUR WARD

Finally, say, "Thank you." You have been given the gift of another day of life and growth, and it is a gift you should never take for granted. No matter what happened in the course of your day, there is reason for gratitude. Look at your cup half-full, not half-empty. Instead of focusing on what you don't have, focus on all the blessings you do have. Thank the universe for all the gifts bestowed upon you. In looking for something to be grateful for, you will find that gratitude arises naturally. Even in the most difficult times, of war, of famine, of sorrow, of death, we can choose to find something to appreciate and be grateful for. The Buddha once told a story of how a traveler came upon a tiger that began to chase him. He ran until he came to an impassible ravine. At the last minute, he spotted a thick vine hanging over the edge of a cliff. He grabbed the vine and swung out over the ravine. *I'm safe!* he thought as he heard the tiger above him snarling and snapping. Then, he heard another roar coming from the ravine. He looked down and saw two more tigers beneath him! He hung suspended on the vine halfway between the tiger at the top of the cliff and the two below.

All of a sudden, he felt a movement on the vine. Two mice had climbed onto the vine and were nibbling on it just out of his reach. He yelled at them, but they continued nibbling. Within minutes, they would gnaw all the way through the vine, and he would fall to his death. Just then, the man noticed that right in front of him hung a beautiful bunch of grapes among the dense vegetation on the cliff. He reached out and plucked two perfectly purple grapes, put them into his mouth, and started to chew. They were the most delicious grapes he had ever tasted!

We all are holding on to the vine of our lives, suspended over the tigers of death with the mice of time gnawing at the vine. Inevitably, time will chew through our lives and we will die. But our days are like those beautiful grapes. If we imbibe them fully, if we are grateful for having them, we can savor our days and make those precious moments joyous and fulfilling. Then our days, which are the gift of time to us, become our gifts back to Essence.

YOUR SOUL'S ENERGY BOOSTERS

- It's not so important to live for today necessarily, but to live in today.
- To make the most of your life, live as if today were your last day on Earth, or the last day of the people you love. Live as if each moment is precious, because it is.
- Start your day with an attitude check, count your blessings.
- Remember the law of attraction: what you focus on creating inside yourself, you will notice or attract more of in the outside world.

- Essence asks us to look for the best in ourselves and others.
- I believe we create our days by the choices we make in every moment.
- We have the choice to look at our problems from a different perspective and to search actively for a meaning that connects us to Essence. Focus on and put love into your tasks and work.
- If you are truly in tune with Essence during your day, you'll find that you often receive messages to guide you.
- End your day with gratitude and reflection.
- You can choose to be and act as your best self. Listen to Essence and listen to your gut instincts.
- Accept what is that you cannot change. This will lessen your suffering. Have faith that what happens ultimately is for the greatest good.

SIX

Understanding Essence to Connect to Spirits and Angels Around You

Man's life does not commence in the womb
and never ends in the grave;
and this firmament, full of moonlight and stars, is
not deserted by loving souls and intuitive spirits.

—KAHLIL GIBRAN

No one walks through this world alone; we are all connected to Essence and its loving force. We are surrounded by Essence in the form of our loved ones, people on Earth, and those who have passed to life on another plane of existence. You can call that plane the *afterlife, the other side, heaven and hell.* But whatever you choose to call it, it exists. It is invisible to us, yet it is where our soul resides and where we spend eternity.

You can think of life on Earth as a term at a boarding school or university. You don't live permanently at school; you stay there while you learn your lessons. You have professors and teachers who guide you. You meet people and make friends, and sometimes form lasting relationships. But eventually you leave school and go back home, where you are surrounded by the family and friends that you have known for years. You reconnect and share with them what you have learned. Then, if you have more lessons to learn, after a while you go back to boarding school or university—hopefully at a higher grade level—and the process of learning and growing begins again. In the university we call *life,* we have many teachers and guides, both seen and unseen, who are here to help us learn and grow. We also have friends, family, and loved ones who have been part of our journey in past lifetimes, or whom we are meeting for the first time. And underlying and overseeing it all is the goodness, wisdom, and love of Essence. Both the changing and the unchanging coexist in Essence. No matter how many lifetimes we go through, how many loved ones enter and exit from our lives, the Essence of our spirits is never lost regardless of the form it takes.

The journey from life on Earth to life on the other side is one of the great mysteries, one that all of us have taken before and will take again. But when the people we love die, it can feel as if our connection is severed. We no longer have the delight of hearing their voice or seeing their beloved face. We cannot hold their hands or feel their caress. Even if we know that their spirits are immortal, our hearts still ache to have them with us on Earth, just for a moment more. But while we miss the physical presence of our dear ones, what we truly love in them is their Essence, which can cross barriers of time, space, and death. We can connect with their Essence at any moment, with our thoughts and prayers. And we can know that their spirits still live, although in a different form, and *we will see our loved ones again.* After more than forty-five years of readings and connecting with thousands of spirits on the other side, I know for a fact that our departed loved ones want to communicate with us and to send us their love. Imagine being a spirit trying to communicate with loved ones who aren't recognizing or listening to them. Imagine how frustrating it is for those souls! My job is to serve as the bridge between the worlds, so your loved ones can connect with us and we can connect with them as well. Our loved ones want us to know that they are all right. They want to continue growing on the other side and help us in our journey through life as we learn and grow, too. And most of all, they will be waiting to welcome us when it's our turn to leave our current "school term" and return home.

The Great Transformation

Death is the veil which those who live call life;
They sleep, and it is lifted.

—PERCY BYSSHE SHELLEY

If you ever have been with someone when they die, you should have little doubt that we are far more than just our physical bodies. Many people say that they could feel the moment when the eternal spark of Essence left the body of the dying person. We leave the pain and struggle of death behind with our physical shell and appear on the other side as we truly are: spirits whose true Essence is light and love. As the spirit, the life force, leaves the body, we see a white light and as we move toward it, we see figures—mother, grandmother, spouse, child, whoever we loved best. They are there to ease our passing and help us become acclimated to our new surroundings. This is a joyous reunion, the best "welcome home" party we could ever imagine.

We also are met by guardian angels and guides who are with us from the moment we're born. They are souls who have grown enough through their lifetimes to be given the responsibility of caring for people on Earth. They are there to watch over us, to protect us, to nudge us in the right direction, to support us as we learn and grow and evolve. They are on our side when we make the right choices, and they pick us up when we fall. Our angels and guides are with us throughout life and at the moment of our death; they are part of the welcoming committee. (Our guardian angels also can watch over the spirits of our loved ones when they pass. Whenever a friend or client tells me that someone they know is dying, I suggest that they ask their guardian angel to meet the spirit when it leaves the body and travels to the other side.)

However, before we move on, we must face a kind of judgment, as the events of our lives pass before our eyes. We see the good deeds we have done and the ones we have failed to do, the effects our choices have had on us and other people, the lessons we have learned and failed to learn. How we have lived will determine what "neighborhood" we will go to on the other side. If we have lived a good life, learned our lessons, and accumulated good karma through our deeds, we will bring all those experiences to the soul (the greater energy that records all our experiences) and go higher. If we have failed to learn our lessons and made choices that have produced hurt, injury, and other bad karma, then our soul is pulled not toward love but further away. We will then need to come back and "repeat the term," so to speak, atoning for the bad karma we created the last time around.

Help and Healing on the Other Side

I shall hear in heaven.

—LUDWIG VAN BEETHOVEN ON HIS DEATHBED

Even though most of us have been incarnated many times, death is often a shock to the system, and some spirits need help to accept and understand their transition. Imagine a spirit encased in a body that has been paralyzed, for example, or in great physical pain, or born with physical or mental disabilities. That person might need some assistance to become accustomed to the freedom of the spirit body, or to allow their mind to catch up to their ethereal body, to realize they are no longer sick, or depressed, or unable to move. In such cases, the spirits will get all the help they need to embrace their new state of freedom and joy. Essence is compassionate and loving, and it takes care of spirits even when they have failed to take care of themselves. Many times when I contact people on the other side who were substance abusers in this lifetime, or who were depressed, or had mental problems, I can sense that they are in the care of spirits that work with them and heal them.

Not long ago, I read for a beautiful but sad older couple whose deceased son, Roy, had a history of emotional problems but refused help. When Roy came through, he apologized profusely to his mom and dad. "Roy wants you to know that he's getting the help he needed on the other side," I told them as they both cried. "He's going through something like a twelve-step program in heaven, and one of the steps is to apologize and ask for forgiveness." A combination of pain, relief, and happiness crossed the faces of both parents. "Roy is grateful that you reached out to him," I said. "He'll be with you anytime you think of him, so send him good thoughts and forgiveness to help him continue to make progress on the other side."

The man who, in a fit of melancholy, kills himself today would have wished to live had he waited a week.

—VOLTAIRE

The saddest spirits I contact are those who have chosen to take their own lives. They may have been overwhelmed by what they were experiencing and saw suicide as the only way out; at other times, factors like drugs or alcohol contributed to their deaths. I remember when I contacted the spirit of a husband who had killed himself while high on cocaine. He came through very clearly to make sure his teenage daughter got the message never to use drugs. Sometimes people who are devastated by a death consider suicide as a way of reuniting with their loved ones on the other side, but this is never the answer. When we make our transition at the time we are destined to, we do so because we have learned our lessons and are ready for our next step. But when people take their own lives, it's kind of like leaving school before the end of the term. Their "classmates"—their loved ones—will move on to the next grade, but they will have to repeat the term and learn the lessons they were meant to before they can advance. When I speak to the spirit of a suicide, I find that most of them hope for understanding and forgiveness from the people they left behind. Once, a young woman, Helen, and her fiancé, Bart, came to see me because her father had killed himself. I picked up on the father's name, Herman, and his father's name as well. "Had your father been ill?" I asked. "I feel that he was on some kind of medication that messed him up. He hit you, didn't he?" Helen looked shocked that I knew.

"He's saying that you were his little girl and he never would have hit you if it hadn't been for the medication," I told her. "He wants you to know that he is so sorry, that he was wrong and in pain. He planned to take his life because he couldn't handle things. You feel guilty because you think you could have saved him, but you couldn't have stopped him even if you'd been here. But now he needs to apologize. Can you accept it?" Helen and Bart embraced and cried as I continued. "Your dad wants you to know that he's watching you and he loves you so much. I feel that he's very happy about this marriage." The young couple left smiling and at peace, and I could feel that her father was more peaceful as well.

Mourning Our Departed Loved Ones

But O for the touch of a vanish'd hand,
And the sound of a voice that is still!

—ALFRED, LORD TENNYSON

Death is a great transition, and it often creates pain—not for those who die but for those who are left behind. Even when we believe in immortality and know in our hearts that our loved ones live on in another place, we still miss them and mourn their loss. There is a story of a master who had taught for many years the Zen Buddhist doctrine that life is an illusion. One day, the master's son died. The students came to see the master and were surprised to see tears coursing down his cheeks. "Master, you weep for your son when you have taught us that life is an illusion?" they asked.

"Yes," the master said, wiping away his tears. "Because he was such a beautiful illusion!"

Grief and mourning are natural expressions at such times, and the rites surrounding someone's passing are important as well. Rituals like funerals and memorial services are helpful not only for the people here but also for the spirits of those who have passed over. Every religious tradition has ways to help us close one chapter of existence and bless our loved ones on their way. Remember, our thoughts and prayers benefit departed spirits. They send the energy of our love to the other side and ease the transition of death. Our thoughts and prayers keep the bridge of love strong and give consolation and strength to both those who are gone and those who are left.

Sometimes the spirits choose to stay close to us after death, making themselves known when we are often the most open emotionally. They may be present at the funeral, sometimes not. They may need time to acclimate to their new surroundings. If their passing was difficult or sudden, they may need some healing on the other side before they can come back. It may be too hard on them to see the grief of the people they have left behind, and their guardian angels will keep them away for a while and let time take the edge off of sorrow. Many times in my readings, however, the spirits tell me details about their funerals or memorial services that help confirm their existence for the people here. One young man told his sister that he had seen her almost fall at his funeral, and it had made him laugh. (His sister exclaimed, "That's just like him!") Another woman said that she had felt an invisible hand rubbing her face very gently at her son's service, and she believed it was her son saying goodbye.

In today's world, it can feel that we want to sweep grief under the rug, but grieving is natural and necessary, and expressing it is important. "To weep is to make less the depth of grief," wrote Shakespeare. "Stuffing" your emotion at such times can keep you from moving through grief to a kind of resolution. However, don't hold on to grief too long. When we lose someone we love, especially if it's a child or someone that was taken at a young age, grief can be all-consuming—and that's not what our loved ones want. I was called to read for a family whose son had drowned in a ditch. "His name began with a *T*, *T-A-R?* Tarik?" I said. "He's telling me he had been drinking for two days and he went out to that spot because he needed some time alone, and then he passed out and fell in the ditch by accident. But he says that it's really difficult to watch you from heaven and see what you're going through." The mother and the sister were crying at this point, but the father was just standing there. "Your son is saying that you cry a lot in private, Dad," I told him. "He doesn't want you to hold it in because it will cause you health problems. He says it's okay to show emotion and to feel, and he wants me to tell you that you were wonderful parents." As all three family members embraced, I could feel Tarik smiling on the other side.

Simply by remembering our loved ones and celebrating their lives, we can connect with their Essence and make them and ourselves happy. Set aside time on birthdays and anniversaries to remember your loved ones. Take a few moments to send them your thoughts and good wishes. If you want, visit their grave or a place that was special to them. Do something that they would have enjoyed doing: if your loved one liked to sail, for example, go sailing, even if you're not fond of the water. Even better, do a good deed in their memory. If you lost a parent, visit an older person who has no family. If you lost a child, maybe there's a single parent who would appreciate an evening where you babysit for their kids, or perhaps there's a shelter that cares for homeless families that would love a contribution or an afternoon of your time. Inscribe the memory of the love you shared upon the hearts of others; it is the best monument your departed loved ones could ever have.

But don't hold on too tightly to their spirits. Remember, our loved ones will continue to grow on the other side, and if we cling to them too tightly, we can keep them tethered to the life they had here and prevent them—and us—from moving on. I saw this with a young mother, Bibi, whose daughter had died very young. "Your great-grandmother is holding your little girl and taking good care of her on the other side," I told Bibi. "I feel her around me, but I'm scared that I'm holding her so she can't go," she said with a sigh. "I want to know if she's with me because she likes it or because I'm keeping her here."

"I think it's a bit of both," I answered as gently as I could. "There's a saying that parents should give their children roots and wings. You've given her roots of love, so let her fly."

Hilary Stanton Zunin once wrote, "The risk of love is loss, and the price of loss is grief—But the pain of grief / Is only a shadow / When compared with the pain / Of never risking love." Love never changes because the energy of love never dies. We never cease to miss our loved ones, but eventually our grief becomes a gentle sorrow as we remember more of the times we had and the love we still can share. Then, whenever we think of our loved ones, we will feel the presence of their Essence.

Guilt and Forgiveness

The bitterest tears shed over graves are for words left unsaid and deeds left undone.

—HARRIET BEECHER STOWE

A lot of us have unresolved issues with our departed loved ones. We think of what we did or failed to do, and we feel we have lost forever our chance to make up for these things. Well, the spirits on the other side feel the same way. In many of my readings, I'm apologizing from the people in heaven to the people living and vice versa. It is natural to have regrets after someone passes over, but such regrets may ease over time as we remember the love we shared. Guilt, on the other hand, is an extremely painful emotion that increases over time. As an Eastern master once taught, "When we are guilty, it is not our sins we hate but ourselves." We feel guilty when we have done something wrong; when we believe we have offended someone and have not taken action to redress the wrong. And when death intervenes before we can atone and ask for forgiveness, guilt can become a burden we carry for the rest of our lives. It can stop everyone, spirits and those who are still here, from moving on.

There's a reason that asking forgiveness and atoning for our transgressions is part of many religions. Asking for forgiveness cleans the slate, so to speak; it eases our burdens, clears our energy, and allows us to connect more completely with Essence. Don't put off asking for forgiveness from those you love while you and they are still on Earth. It may not be easy to admit your mistakes or errors, but you don't want to have such things on your conscience when you pass over. If you feel that you need to ask forgiveness from someone who has passed over, you can do so by utilizing the same kind of intuitive connection described in chapters 3 and 4.

ASKING FORGIVENESS FROM THOSE YOU HAVE LOST

Close your eyes, surround yourself with white light, and then connect with Essence. Then bring the image of your loved one into your mind and heart. Connect with them by sending them love, and then tell them how sorry you are for whatever you did or failed to do. With humility, ask for their forgiveness. Notice any thoughts, images, feelings, or emotions that come up that may be signs from your loved one that they have accepted your apology.

Remember, your departed loved ones do not lose their personalities on the other side, so if they were not forgiving people while they were here, it may take a while before they forgive you. But keep at it. Making the request and asking for forgiveness will go a long way to healing your own inner guilt whether your apology is accepted or not. And also be aware that if you are asking for forgiveness for actions that you are still taking, that's not a genuine request. If you were verbally abusive to someone before they died and you still abuse the people in your life, you will continue to accumulate the bad karma of the abuse no matter how many times you ask forgiveness from both the living and the dead. Ask to be forgiven and change your ways for the better. That is the only sign of true atonement.

Forgiveness is the giving, and so the receiving, of life.

—GEORGE MACDONALD

I can't stress enough how important it is to clean things up with your loved ones before they pass away. In reading after reading, the spirits of fathers, mothers, brothers, sisters, friends, and family of all kinds come through because they want to apologize and ask for our forgiveness. I have seen and felt their pain and the pain of the people they left behind; I also have seen the relief and peace that occurs when a connection is made and relationships are healed. One day, a mother and daughter took me to the spot where the father had burned to death in a trailer fire. "His name was Willem," I told them. "And recently you were saying some harsh things about him.

But he says, 'You told the truth. I really messed up your lives, financially and in matters of the heart.'" I could feel Willem's desire for his family's forgiveness. I turned to the mother. "This is your chance to help him grow in the spirit world and become a kinder spirit. He says that if he could do it all over again, he'd be nicer to you. And he wants you to tell your son, Stefan, that Willem apologizes to him, too. He was not a good role model for his son."

Not long ago, another family asked me for a reading. The father had died eight years earlier, and when the sister was nine months pregnant, her oldest brother was killed in an automobile accident. I picked up on the brother's name, Ismail, as well as his grandmother and father, who were looking out for him on the other side. "Did you have a ceremony for him with all his friends there? And did people put his favorite things in with him, including his favorite foods? He's telling me that that made him laugh because most people wouldn't have done that. He's asking about a *T*, Tim?"

"That's the driver of the car that hit my brother," the sister answered.

"Have you forgiven Tim yet?" I asked. There was a moment of silence. "Your brother wants you to forgive Tim," I insisted. "It was just an accident, and it was Ismail's time. He's happy in heaven, and he's saying, 'Forgive Tim, because I've forgiven him.'"

> We all love best not those who offend us least, nor those who have done most for us, but those who make it most easy for us to forgive them.
>
> —SAMUEL BUTLER

Forgiveness is one of the highest and best gifts we can bestow on people here and hereafter. However, forgiveness doesn't mean becoming a doormat and allowing yourself to be abused, and it certainly doesn't mean condoning abusive behavior toward yourself or others. On the other hand, holding on to hatred and failing to forgive those who ask it of us hurts us far more than the one who sinned in the first place. As the Buddha once said, it's like grasping a hot coal thinking that you're going to throw it at an offender, but you're the one that gets burned. Recognize that you can forgive the sinner and still hate the behavior, and your forgiveness may give this person the space to choose to follow a higher path. The ability to forgive is a key component of love, and thus it should be an ability we use whenever possible. Forgiving others makes it easier to forgive ourselves. Try to offer the blessing of forgiveness when it is requested, and to practice forgiveness for yourself and others.

Sending and Receiving Love

Wear not the black of mourning
But rejoice with me in white raiment.
Speak not in sorrow of my going
But close your eyes and you shall see me among you,
Now and forevermore.

—KAHLIL GIBRAN

Connecting with our loved ones on the other side is simple; it's done with thought, with prayer, with attention, and most of all, with love. Love is the bridge that connects us to the spirit world. The energy of love is powerful and healing on the spirit plane as well as here, and we can send our love to those who have passed over, simply by thinking of them. Thoughts are things; thoughts have power. They are an instant bridge to the other side.

CONNECT WITH A DEPARTED LOVED ONE THROUGH MEMORY

If you wish to feel the presence of a departed love one, bring a particularly good memory of them to mind. Create it as fully as possible for yourself. How did your loved one look, sound, move, smell? (Fragrances are some of our strongest memories—a loved one's aftershave or perfume, or the smell of a little baby, for instance.) Feel what you felt when you were with them, and feel the emotions they had as well. Send that person your love, and listen for any message they may have for you. Another way to connect is to go to a park, for example, sit on a bench, think of that person you want to connect with, and have a chat with them. By doing so, you're bringing their Essence back. It's simple and easy to do, but it can be profound.

When you bring a loved one into your mind, it's like picking up the phone and dialing. You're sending out a call with your loving thoughts. Sometimes our loved ones will use our thoughts to let us know they are around and sending us love. Have you ever been at home or doing something that doesn't take your full attention, and all of a sudden for no particular reason you think about your grandmother, or parent, or friend, or spouse, or child, or anyone who has died? It may be that the spirit of that person wants to say hello. Prayer is also a powerful way to connect with our loved ones. You may light a candle, connect in your heart with the eternal love of Essence, and then bring your loved one into your prayers. Ask for Essence to hold your loved one with love and bless them. Pray for them to continue to grow in light and love.

Often our loved ones devise all kinds of ways to communicate. Remember, each spirit retains its unique energy thumbprint, its personality, on the other side. When our departed loved ones come through, we can still identify them as spouse, child, parent, grandparent, or friend. Not long ago, a man who died in a sailing accident during a race came through to speak to his wife. "Did he have a good sense of humor?" I asked her. "He's telling me, 'Just because I fell off the boat doesn't mean I lost the race.'"

Our departed loved ones use many signs and signals to let us know they are still connected with us. All birds (especially hummingbirds), butterflies, feathers, and other natural phenomena are common. As are coins. So are noises and other strange events close to the time of someone's death. One woman who had passed very suddenly—while she was on the telephone with her best friend, Carolyn—was trying very hard to communicate with her mother on this side. "I see her pounding on things, trying to make noise to reach you," I said. "And she also did something with a clock."

"Funny you should say that," Carolyn replied. "I've heard inexplicable noises in my friend's house, and her mother's watch stopped at the exact time her daughter died."

Many spirits seem to find it easy to manipulate electricity—not surprising, as electricity is a form of energy. After a death, people will report that lights either flicker or go on and off completely without anyone being near the light switch. One woman who had lost her father told me that when she and her fiancé started to make wedding plans, a light outside their house went on and off. "I went to check on it, and it wasn't even plugged in," she said.

"Your father is signaling that he's happy about your marriage," I told her.

Children have a pure energy, and they are more open to sense the Essence of our departed loved ones. If you have a child in the family that talks about seeing their grandmother or grandfather, or hearing from a departed brother or sister or parent or friend, don't negate their experience or tell them that they're mistaken; listen to them and see what they have to say. Sometimes these beautiful little souls are clear channels that help us hear messages from those who are gone. I heard recently from Greta, who lost her dearly beloved brother, that she was often astounded to hear her young son use expressions that only her dead brother used in life. "My boy is too young to remember my brother," Greta commented. "But it's just as if my brother were whispering in his ear."

In the same way that Essence can speak to us through our dreams, our loved ones also can use this channel to communicate. In dreaming, the conscious mind is put aside and we are open to messages from beyond. A mother who lost her daughter in an automobile accident dreamed that her daughter drove up to the front door. "I said to her, 'But we buried you!'" the mother told me. "And she said, 'You can see it's not true—I'm here.'"

"That was her way of telling you that she's okay and she has a new life in heaven. She's with her grandmother and is preparing a home for each of you when you go to heaven. But that's going to be a long time!" I reassured the mother.

> If we all discovered that we had only five minutes left to say all that we wanted to say, every telephone booth would be occupied by people calling other people to tell them that they loved them.
>
> —CHRISTOPHER MORLEY

Love never dies, and our loved ones in spirit will go to great lengths to let us know how much they care. If nothing else, this fact should move us all to take every opportunity to connect with our loved ones on Earth, to tell them how important they are and how much we cherish them. It also should propel us to clean up our relationships. Don't let things fester; make your peace while they are here rather than having to live in regret after they are gone because you didn't say what needed to be said. Embrace your dear ones while they are here. When they go, you will remember the feeling of their embrace, every expression of love, and so will they. Such moments of shared love are the only things we can take with us when we die. They will help those of us left behind to remember that death is only a temporary, physical separation, that love is stronger than death, and we can always connect with those we love—spirit to spirit, Essence to Essence, heart to heart.

YOUR SOUL'S ENERGY BOOSTERS

- We are surrounded by Essence in the form of our loved ones, people on Earth, and those who have passed to life on another plane of existence.
- In the university we call life, we have many teachers and guides, both seen and unseen who are here to help us learn and grow.
- While we miss the physical presence of our loved one when they cross over what we truly love in them is the energy of their Essence, which can cross barriers of time, space, and death.
- When we cross over, we are met by loved ones, guardian angels and spirit guides to ease our passing.
- Before we move on to the spirit world, we judge ourselves in the eyes of divine love.

- Grieving is natural and necessary, and expressing it is important.
- Simply by remembering our loved ones and celebrating their lives, we connect with their Essence and make them and ourselves happy.
- Don't hold on to our deceased loved ones too tightly. We can prevent them from moving on to their greater purpose.
- Asking forgiveness and atoning for our transgressions helps us and our loved ones heal.
- Connecting with our loved ones on the other side is simple; it's done with thought, with prayer, with attention, and most of all with love.
- Love never dies, and our loved ones will go to great lengths to let us know how much they care.

SEVEN

Good and Evil: The Essential Paradox

We cannot freely and wisely choose the right way for ourselves unless we know both good and evil.

—HELEN KELLER

If the underlying energy of everything in the universe is Essence, which is goodness, love, and wisdom, then how can such energy be turned into the pain, violence, and cruelty we see all too frequently in the news and in our lives? How can a loving and caring Essence condone such things as genocide, murder, or abuse? If God is good, then why is there evil? Humanity has been wrestling with such questions ever since ancient times. Good and evil seem to be a part of the fabric of the universe. But how can that be, if the ultimate goodness of Essence is our fundamental nature? I'm not a philosopher, but I have come to realize the world runs like a battery, there is always a positive and negative charge. I don't know for sure why we have good and evil in the world or in the afterlife, but I've come to believe and accept two things. First, maybe somehow we need duality—both the energy of good and its opposite—for the world to exist at all. After all, creation as described in the book of Genesis arises from duality, opposites, heaven and earth, light and dark. "In the beginning God created the heaven and the earth. And the earth was without form, and void; and darkness was upon the face of the deep. . . . And God said, Let there be light: and there was light. And God saw the light, that it was good: and God divided the light from the darkness." (Genesis 1:1–4) Without light, how could we know darkness? Without darkness, how would we know light? In the Chinese tradition, yin, the bright male energy, needs yang, the dark female energy, for creation. Maybe what we see as opposites in the energy of the universe are instead complements, two halves of the same whole, and both are necessary to keep the world in existence. As Deepak Chopra comments, "If there were only truth, goodness, harmony, and beauty, the universe would expand and disappear. There has to be something to hold it back."

I think there is the same dynamic tension inside every human being. I certainly don't ascribe to the idea that human beings are fundamentally flawed because we chose to disobey God back in the Garden of Eden. But I do believe that human beings have inside themselves the potential for both good and evil. Yes, our Essence is goodness, love, and wisdom, but if every energy in the universe holds within itself the potential for its opposite, then human beings are no different. Doesn't every emotion have a light and dark side? Love can become jealousy, goodness can become self-righteousness, wisdom can become dogmatism, and peace can become fear of conflict. Along with love, wisdom, peace, and goodness, we also possess the potential for hatred, cruelty, anger, selfishness, violence, arrogance, and disregard for others. Carl Jung called such traits our *shadow,* the aspects of our personalities that we do not wish to acknowledge or let out, but that can cause great internal harm if they are unacknowledged or ignored.

However, here is the underlying truth about human beings, the eternal truth that is symbolized in the story of Adam and Eve in the garden: *at every moment, we have the opportunity to choose between goodness and its opposite.* It reminds me of one of my favorite Cherokee legends.

> *An old Cherokee is teaching his grandson about life. "A fight is going on inside me," he said to the boy. "It is a terrible fight and it is between two wolves. One is evil—he is anger, envy, sorrow, regret, greed, arrogance, self-pity, guilt, resentment, inferiority, lies, false pride, superiority, and ego."*
>
> *He continued, "The other is good—he is joy, peace, love, hope, serenity, humility, kindness, benevolence, empathy, generosity, truth, compassion, and faith. The same fight is going on inside you—and inside every other person, too."*
>
> *The grandson thought about it for a minute and then asked his grandfather, "Which wolf will win?"*
>
> *The old Cherokee simply replied, "The one you feed."*

Free will means that we are free to choose the path and actions that take us closer or draw us further away from Essence. We can choose to be hurtful, cruel, callous, violent, deceitful, prejudiced, and hateful. We can choose not to see the value and goodness in other people or in ourselves. Most of us may have inadvertently or accidentally taken such actions at some point and felt their effects. However, we also can choose to grow closer to Essence instead by doing good, being loving, helping others, telling the truth—all the virtues taught in cultures around the world. With every choice, we are setting a direction for our lives that will have a significant impact, not merely today but for lifetimes to come. Our incarnations are designed to test us, to bring us up against challenges, and to help teach us to use the incredible power of our free will. Part of our responsibility on Earth is to make the best possible choices we can, to learn the lessons that bring us closer to Essence. If the only choice possible were goodness, where would the growth be in that?

> **Life in itself is neither good nor evil; it is the scene of good or evil, as you make it.**
>
> —MONTAIGNE

Perhaps our lifetimes on Earth mirror the progress we see in ourselves as we grow from babies to adulthood. When we are babies, our parents take care of all our needs. We don't have to make decisions; we simply express our desires, and "goodness"—the people who love us—fills them. But as we grow bigger, we discover that we can do things for ourselves. We start to crawl, then walk, then run; we go from being breastfed to spoon-fed to feeding ourselves. We start to want to make decisions and have input in our lives—what toy to play with, what to wear, when to go to bed. There's a sense of both joy and power in the ability to make choices, but there is also the responsibility to learn the effects of our choices on ourselves and others. If we choose to take a toy away from a playmate, what happens? The other child cries or perhaps hits us. If we give the toy we're playing with to someone else, what result does that create? The other child may invite us to play. If we had no choice in the matter, if we could *only* choose the good, would we learn the same lessons? Of course not. Only babies and those with limited capacity need their choices made for them. Being able to choose good or evil, having the free will to say yes or no to the apple in the Garden of Eden, is what makes us grow to become the beautiful, Essence-like souls that ultimate goodness wishes us to be.

Growing and learning also means that we must learn to understand and accept paradox, the dynamic tension between opposites, in the world and within ourselves. We must accept the fact that there is darkness within, that we all have the potential for evil actions. We must acknowledge the dark emotions that are part of our nature and we are capable of doing great harm to ourselves and others. We have to recognize our tendencies and then choose another way. We must accept the parts of ourselves that do not resonate with the highest and forgive ourselves for our failings while always striving to do better. We said in an earlier chapter, we must hate the sin and love the sinner, and we must do that with ourselves before we can do it with others. We must love all the parts of ourselves, even those parts that have the potential of darkness, while resolving to choose to do only good. To embrace our darkness without acting upon it is a key step in becoming like Essence. When we can recognize and forgive the presence of darkness in ourselves, it makes it possible to do the same with others. We do not accept or condone evil, and we do our best to strive against it whenever we encounter it, but we begin to understand and have compassion for the one who commits the sin. "Judge not, that ye be not judged," Jesus said in the Sermon on the Mount. When we recognize that we, too, have potential for evil, we can move from judgment to understanding, vengeance to forgiveness, from hatred to compassion. Stepping out of judgment gives us the freedom to choose another way.

A large part of our progress here on Earth comes from recognizing evil, turning away from it, and choosing good instead. The person who goes through life without temptation may have a good life and go to a great neighborhood when they pass over, but how much more progress will be made by those who are challenged by many temptations, who have to fight evil, and who manage to overcome and do good even in the most difficult circumstances? We have the power to shape our lives by the choices we make, and at any moment we can change the direction of our lives and turn from evil to good. As the prophet Muhammad wrote, "Every human being has two inclinations—one prompting him to good . . . and the other prompting him to evil . . . but Divine assistance is near, and he who asks the help of God in contending with the evil promptings of his own heart obtains it." There are countless stories of men and women who did horrible things when they were younger but who became saints and role models. Saint Francis was a dissolute young nobleman until he gave everything away to become a wandering friar. Bill Wilson was a hopeless drunk until one day he had an experience of God and never touched another drink. He went on to cofound Alcoholics Anonymous, which has helped millions of people battle alcoholism.

I think that some older souls are given the greatest challenges. It's as if there is an Olympics of good and evil, and to face its greatest foes Essence only puts in its top players who have the most strength and skill. If you find yourself faced with great challenges, remember that, as Mother Teresa said, "I know God will not give me anything I can't handle." (Of course, she added, "I just wish that he didn't trust me so much.") Sometimes we must call upon our strength to face down evil when it appears. We must be strong enough to say no to the temptation to do evil, to take the easy way out, or to act for our own benefit if it harms others. And we must be strong enough to challenge the evil in the actions of others. As Martin Luther King, Jr. reminds us, "He who passively accepts evil is as much involved in it as he who helps to perpetrate it. He who accepts evil without protesting against it is really cooperating with it." When we stand up to evil, we must remember that *good is always stronger than evil in the long run.* It can take a lot of good to overcome evil, in the same way it takes many coats of white paint to cover just one coat of black. However, there is power to be had in aligning ourselves with the forces of good, inside ourselves and in the outside world. When we stand up to evil, we are tapping into the power of universal goodness, which provides Essence its strength.

Good and Evil from the Eternal Viewpoint

There is no explanation for evil. It must be looked upon as a necessary part of the order of the universe. To ignore it is childish; to bewail it senseless.

—W. SOMERSET MAUGHAM

When faced with evil, we also must remember another fact that helps us make sense of the paradox of a fundamentally good universe allowing evil to exist: *this lifetime is only one stage of eternity.* While we are on Earth, we cannot see the whys and wherefores of karma and destiny. We cannot understand the forces that would allow murder, abuse, genocide, and destruction. Here on Earth, we cannot see the eternal justice that rewards good and punishes evil; that is what we see when we pass over to the other side. There we can begin to understand why events on Earth unfold the way they do, and how our individual lifetimes fit into the upward spiral of souls and spirits learning and growing and becoming one with Essence.

After forty-five years speaking with spirits on the other side and feeling the energy of those who are in good neighborhoods and those in bad, I can say with confidence that there is *always* justice and repayment for transgressions and deeds of evil. If justice doesn't happen in this lifetime, it will occur on the other side and in the next. As I mentioned, there are "neighborhoods" of different energies where our spirits go after death, depending on our actions on Earth. If someone has been cruel or caused great harm here, that spirit would not resonate with a neighborhood of goodness, so it will end up in a lower neighborhood where it will have to learn some potentially difficult lessons before it can progress. These lower neighborhoods are not pleasant. Just as we can make our own hell on Earth, we make our own hell on the other side. I'm not speaking of the fires of hell; the pain of the spirits in these neighborhoods instead comes from seeing and feeling the pain they caused others while on Earth. Imagine abusers or murderers who have to go through the physical and emotional pain their victims felt—perhaps that's the real meaning behind "an eye for an eye." They also have the pain of seeing how they could have made better choices that would have allowed them to grow in goodness, wisdom, and love. Seeing and feeling the consequences of bad choices, on others as well as ourselves, is some of the worst pain we can experience—the pain of opportunities forever lost. After time in these lower neighborhoods, the spirits reincarnate so they will have a chance to make amends and to choose good over evil. But they do have to suffer from the bad karma they created in their previous lives. What goes around comes around, dictating the circumstances we find ourselves in during our lifetime.

The good news is that every lifetime we have the chance to help those on the other side who are in the bad neighborhoods. If you have a loved one who did wrong either to themselves or to others, pray for them. Send them your loving energy. Your thoughts and prayers will help them learn their lessons and raise their energy so they can atone for their deeds more quickly. They still will have to face the karma they have created when they come back to Earth, but your thoughts and prayers can help make it easier for them to learn their lessons and grow. The good and evil that we choose to do on Earth is truly an eternal legacy, one that will shape our lives both here and in the hereafter. Whenever you are faced with evil or the temptation to do wrong, remember that your choice in this moment is pointing you in one direction or the other, toward good or toward its opposite. Trickster energies are known to distract us from achieving our accomplishments towards success and our goals. So it is wise for all of us to be aware because it can fool us and take us off our path of goodness.

When "Do No Evil" has been understood,
Then learn the harder, braver rule, "Do Good."

—ARTHUR GUITERMAN

WHAT GOOD WILL I DO / HAVE I DONE?

Benjamin Franklin was known for his aphorisms and advice on living virtuously. According to reports, he awoke each day and asked himself, "What good will I do this day?" In the evening, as he got into bed, he asked, "What good have I done this day?" These two questions helped him focus his efforts on goodness and accomplishment. Try asking yourself these questions, morning and night, and see how they shape your day.

Spirits of Goodness and Evil

Millions of spiritual Creatures walk the Earth
Unseen, both when we wake, and when we sleep.

—JOHN MILTON, *PARADISE LOST*

Just as there is yin and yang, there are good and bad energies in the universe, spirits and energies that are no longer attached to bodies but are present on Earth just the same. The good energies help elevate us and inspire us to learn and grow in love and wisdom. The bad energies want to frighten us (because it's their job; our job is to not allow it to affect us), to trick us into taking action that creates bad karma. Both good and bad energies can attach themselves to people and locations here on Earth as well as on the other side. Have you ever gone into a church or sacred site and felt an energy of goodness and holiness? You may be sensing the presence of good spirits and angels. I believe that some of the shrines where people experience healings have angels in attendance, to hear the prayers of the faithful and grant their requests for blessings and good health. On the other hand, there are places where you can feel bad energy. At the concentration camps of the Nazis, the residue left by the cruel deaths of millions of people permeates the grounds and fills the air. Few people can visit such sites and not be affected deeply. Other locations are home to what I call *trickster energies,* low-level spirits who want to pull us away from good and toward the bad. They use misdirection and do their best to make us believe the worst about ourselves and others. Being around such spirits for any length of time can have a horrendous effect on both our bodies and our souls, making us feel depressed, angry, sad, or fearful. Earlier you heard about a woman whose father had committed suicide. We went together to the apartment where her father had lived. "I came here a few months ago with my husband, and as soon as I went into the living room, I felt nauseous," she said to me as we climbed the stairs to his apartment. I looked out the window of the living room—there was a cemetery right next door. I felt nauseous, too, and we left the house quickly. Once outside, we both felt better. I told the woman, "There are trickster spirits that are attached to the cemetery. They are trying to upset you and make you think that your dad was evil, but it's not true. Put a white light of protection around yourself whenever you feel this kind of energy again, and send your dad lots of healing energy on the other side."

Like attracts like, and people who are attuned to dark energies or going through difficult times, like this woman's father, can sometimes find themselves drawn to places with negative energy. And because at such times we are emotionally vulnerable, the negative energies can take advantage of us and pull us into their darkness more easily. That's why we have to be so careful of our energy, especially when we are experiencing negative emotions. If ever you find yourself depressed, or angry, or having feelings of violence for no reason when you go in a house or enter a place you've never been before, or you feel physically ill, you may be encountering a trickster spirit. Put the brightest white light around yourself, say a prayer of protection, send the energy back to where it came from, and get out of there. Even if your emotions weren't due to a spirit, surrounding yourself with white light will help you elevate your energy and perhaps ease your negative feelings. For extra protection, I visualize a mirror in front of me as I wrote in my book *Questions From Earth, Answers From Heaven*. Or better yet, use the mirrored egg that my friend Patti Negri shared with me.

Luckily, there are good energies that surround us and wish us well. We already spoke of our guardian angels and guiding spirits. They are with us frequently, as are other good spirits that come to the earth to help us all. Mary Baker Eddy wrote, "When angels visit us, we do not hear the rustle of wings, nor feel the feathery touch of the breast of a dove; but we know their presence by the love they create in our hearts." When you feel love for no particular reason, you may be near an angel or good spirit, perhaps even the spirit of a departed loved one. Say hello and send them your love in return. Ask these spirits and angels for help, but always connect with Essence first. This will ensure that the spirits you sense are of the highest.

Protecting Yourself from Negative Energy

IMPORTANT EXERCISE TO PROTECT YOURSELF

Imagine the depths of your soul's brightest light illuminating to the outside of your body as if you are lit up by the sun and surrounded by its rays. Swirl those lights around you like a funnel of protective energy. Then put yourself inside a mirrored egg and close it up tight. You are safe inside the egg. The shell of the egg is a mirror so anything negative coming toward you will bounce back to where it came from. Recite: "Anything that is in, near, around, or about me that is not of light go back to where you came from and if you choose to, turn to light." This will help protect you. Once you are safe inside your egg, you can put your loved ones in their own protective mirrored egg.

Angels and ministers of grace, defend us!

—WILLIAM SHAKESPEARE, *HAMLET*

If you feel that you are being faced with evil or negative energies, make it a priority to protect your Essence. White light is like a protective shield that keeps out negative energy. It also illuminates your surroundings and can reveal anything that may be trying to do you harm. The more you allow this goodness to permeate your body, the more it can protect you. The other powerful means of protection is through prayer. I have one that I have used for twenty-five years at the start of every reading. It asks Essence to guide and protect us as we tap into the wisdom of the universe and state our pure intention to spread love and heal life in this world and the next. You are welcome to create your own version of this prayer, or use a prayer or mantra that you're familiar with, such as the rosary, or the Lord's Prayer, or anything else that has meaning for you. Or you can simply close your eyes, connect with Essence, and ask for its protection. It's also good to call on your guardian angels and guides to be with you anytime you feel negative energy around you. Remember, we control spirits and the energies that may surround us; they do not control us unless we give them the power to do so. *No one, on Earth or in spirit, has power over us unless we give it to them.* That's why it's so important to keep your focus on the good, remember your Essence, and recognize your power to direct your actions and your life. That power often includes taking practical action to fight evil. There's a story about a woman who was complaining angrily to God about all the poverty and distress in the world. "Why do you let this happen?" she cried. "Why don't you do something?"

"I did," God answered. "I made you."

We are the hands of good in the battle against evil, so we must be willing to stand up to evil and say no, to challenge evil and stop it from acting in our lives as well as the lives of others. We must be willing to do what it takes to protect ourselves from those who would do us harm. There was a woman whose father came through in a reading who was checking out his daughter's current romance. "This man in your life—Thomas—was your husband when your dad was alive," I said. "You divorced him, but now he's back. Your dad wants Thomas to know that he's going to have to prove that he regrets having hurt you and cheated on you. Your dad says you're too trusting, and you will have to tell Thomas that one bad move and he's out." Good should never allow itself to be a doormat for evil. That's not what Essence wants for us, and it certainly doesn't elevate the level of goodness in the world. We must be willing to stand and fight on the side of the angels and be strong.

Fear and Essence

Only a fool is never afraid.

—RON MEYER

While many of us would classify fear as a negative or dark emotion, it has a valuable purpose. Fear can be a warning that something is wrong. It can signal the presence of danger. It tips us off to potential problems or negative energies. It can let us know we are venturing into unknown territory. It can even be enjoyable; that's why roller coasters and scary movies are so popular. Fear can tell us that we need to prepare, or summon our courage and act, or warn others and run. Fear can protect us, or it can keep us from doing and giving our best. Fear can block us from experiencing or listening to Essence. It can separate us from the knowledge of who we truly are. But fear also can cause us to call upon a power greater than ourselves for help. All of us can experience moments of fear; the difficulties arise when fear becomes an ongoing part of our lives, or when fear appears for no reason, or if it stops us from acting.

Good fear warns us, tips us off, and gets us to take action. You're walking down the street and you feel a sense of fear arise for no reason, so you cross to the other side. Then around the corner comes a dangerous-looking man. Your fear tipped you off to potential danger even before you could see it consciously. That's good fear. Good fear makes us stop and think and prepare. On the other hand, bad fear incapacitates us and keeps us from acting when we should. Bad fear often arises from a sense of our limitations. Imagine you're asked to give a speech at an annual conference. You've never given a speech to a large, prestigious group, but it's an important career move, so you accept. As soon as the word *yes* leaves your mouth, you're terrified. Bad fear makes you say to yourself, "I can't do this!" Bad fear causes you to write draft after draft of the speech, rejecting each because it isn't good enough. Bad fear keeps you up at night worrying, or creates dreams about standing in front of the audience in your underwear. Bad fear prevents you from drawing upon your resources and keeps you from preparing adequately. Ultimately, bad fear might be a self-fulfilling prophecy—you really can't make the speech because you are so afraid. Bad fear drains and exhausts us. It can blind you to the information you may need. If you live in fear constantly, you will never know when intuition is tipping you off. At its worst, bad fear continues to affect us even when the situation changes. Someone who has been mugged, for example, may be afraid to walk down the street alone even if it's the middle of the day in a safe neighborhood. Bad fear often has little to no basis in reality. As Samuel Butler wrote, "Fear is static that prevents me from hearing myself." Bad fear makes us forget the enormous resources of emotion and intellect that we possess. Worst of all, bad fear can cut us off from the source of our most profound strength, the Essence that is within.

When you come up against fear, first you must use your logic and common sense to see if it's a valid response to the situation. If you're in a potentially dangerous part of town, logic and common sense will tell you that fear is probably a smart reaction. The first time you attempt something, for example, it's natural to have some mild fear, which can turn quickly into excitement if you simply take things step by step. Ask yourself, *What's the source of this fear? Is there a logical reason that I'm uneasy?* If your fear is due to something that any reasonable human being would understand, then your fear is a signal either to (1) change your circumstances, or (2) prepare. If you're driving down a street and a big car comes barreling toward you in the wrong lane, logic and common sense will tell you to change your circumstances as quickly as possible! It's also possible that your fear is a signal to prepare. Remember the example of being asked to give a speech? Your fear is a signal that you need to prepare thoroughly. So you write out your speech and practice it until you're completely comfortable with what you have to say. The day of the conference, you walk onstage with confidence, your fear reduced to butterflies in your stomach and a pleasurable sense of anticipation.

If your fear seems to come from something other than logic or common sense, then you need to draw upon your connection to the inner wisdom of Essence to discover what to do. Intuitive fear arises from deep within. It can be a niggling sense that something's not quite right, or a strong certainty of imminent danger. There's a reason we call such fears *gut instinct*—we usually feel them in the pit of the stomach, or somewhere in the vicinity of the heart. We ignore intuitions of fear at our peril, because they are Essence trying to keep us safe from either harm or a bad choice. Perhaps you've been seeing someone and the relationship is getting serious, but something about the relationship makes you nervous (another word for *fear*). You ignore your feelings and move in together, only to find out that your lover is cheating on you. If you'd listened to your intuitive fears, you might have saved yourself a lot of heartache. Whenever a fear arises that can't be explained by logic or common sense, or if the sensation of fear is almost pre-thought, coming from the body rather than the mind, put a white light of protection around yourself and ask Essence what message this fear has for you. When it comes to preventing problems and saving us from harm, the messages from our intuition are just as valuable, if not more, than what logic and common sense can tell us.

> Fear is a kind of bell, or gong, which rings the mind into quick life and avoidance upon the approach of danger. It is the soul's signal for rallying.
>
> —HENRY WARD BEECHER

In other circumstances, you may feel fear because you're stepping out of your comfort zone. Expansion is the fundamental nature of Essence, and therefore it's our nature, too. In every moment, we can choose to create something better, something new, to expand, or we can stay where we are. Unfortunately, because the nature of Essence is to expand, if we stay the same, it's like contracting: the world grows around us and we occupy less and less space within it. Human beings can find change intimidating, and many of us develop areas where we feel safe because they are familiar. Some people have a fear of success and sabotage the opportunity for themselves. Even when we become uncomfortable within it, we rarely step outside of a comfort zone—as an old proverb says, "Better the devil you know than the devil you don't know." Fear of leaving a comfort zone has kept many people in abusive relationships and dead-end jobs. Thousands of human beings fail to go after what they want simply because every time they take the first step outside of what they know, they feel fear. So they keep walking around in the same old comfort zone until it becomes a rut. And, as someone once told me, if you keep walking around a rut, eventually it is as deep as a grave.

The kind of fear that keeps us stuck in a comfort zone is based upon one of two false assumptions. First, we are afraid that we are not enough and we don't have the ability to handle a new situation. We don't feel we have the experience, or the resources, or the emotional strength to deal with what lies outside. We are stuck in a limited view of ourselves and our abilities. We are forgetting that we have within us all the resources, all the strength, all the power of the universe. In Essence, we are always enough, and we can handle anything that Essence brings our way. The second fear is simply the fear of the unknown. We have no confidence or certainty about the outcome of stepping out of our comfort zone and into something new. We are buying into the illusion that we can *ever* know what's going to happen! The only true certainty in life is that things will change, so trying to hold on to things as they are is impossible. We're better off embracing the gifts of the unknown instead of resisting the inevitability of change.

Katharine Butler Hathaway was disabled from spinal tuberculosis at an early age, yet she became a writer and member of the New York literary scene in the 1920s. She said, "If you let fear of consequence prevent you from following your deepest instinct, then your life will be safe, expedient, and thin." Hathaway never let fear of consequence keep her from doing what she wanted with her life, and neither should we. I believe fear that is not a warning of an obvious, imminent danger is a signal to take a look at what's really going on. If you have examined your fear in the light of logic, common sense, and intuition, and you can find no real reason for your fear, then it's time to be honest with yourself. Is fear your usual response to a situation? Are you afraid because you are focused on difficult events from your past? (If so, please consider getting counseling or other psychological assistance to handle the trauma.) Is there a valid reason for your fear, or are you simply afraid of change, failure, or the unknown? Are you caught up in the trap of what-ifs? *What if I fail? What if this doesn't turn out well? What if I lose my money or my job? What if they reject me?* If any of these questions come up, you are trapped in a comfort zone. Honesty is the first step outside of a comfort zone and into the expanded life that Essence wants for us all.

WHAT'S THE WORST THAT COULD HAPPEN?

If you find yourself asking what-if questions, follow them up by asking yourself, *What's the worst that could happen?* What's the worst that could happen if you did fail? What's the worst that could happen if it didn't turn out well, or if you lost your money or your job, or if they rejected you? Could you handle the consequences, even if they were difficult? Asking this question can help you recognize the truth that dispels fear.

On the other hand, what's the *best* that could happen? What would happen if you challenged your fear and took action? How much would you grow? What could you gain even if the worst occurred? You are much more than any circumstance that you may face. Have the courage to step over your fears, out of your comfort zone, and into an expanded life.

Four Options for Dealing with Fear

To conquer fear is the beginning of wisdom.

—BERTRAND RUSSELL

Once you determine the roots of your fear, you have a choice about how to deal with them. First, you can do nothing and hope the situation changes. In some cases, this is a valid response. When certain animals in the wild sense a predator, they will stand absolutely still and blend in to their surroundings. In some situations, you need the will and courage to endure and outlast the fear. Think of the people who are caught in war zones or in natural disasters like hurricanes. When you've done everything you can and the storm is whirling or the bombs are dropping outside, all you can do is stay put and have the courage to endure your circumstances until they change.

In most cases, however, fear is a signal that we must either "fly"—move—or turn and fight. You've heard about the flight-or-fight impulse that is present in most living creatures. Fear compels us either to get ourselves out of the situation or to turn and fight.

The second option in dealing with fear is to take action to get us out of fear. This doesn't necessarily mean leaving the context in which you are feeling fearful; more often, it means moving something within ourselves—that is, making a change. If you want a better job but you're afraid to leave your current one, you will need to do something to increase your confidence. This might include creating a six-month job-seeking plan, getting some additional training to prepare you for a better position, hiring a career counselor to advise you on your job search, and so on. If you're worried about your health, fear won't do you any good unless it moves you to get to the gym or the doctor or to change unhealthy habits. Whenever you are faced with a fear, ask yourself, *What do I need to do differently to eliminate this fear and feel good in this particular area?* And then make it a priority to take at least one step toward the change you wish to make. Taking the first step often will ease your fears enough that the next steps will be easier.

The third option is to turn and fight, to make a stand and oppose whatever is causing your fear, whether it's your outer circumstances or the circumstances inside. If you're afraid to ask that good-looking person out on a date, face your fear and pick up the phone. If you've always wanted to be a doctor or lawyer or salesperson or potter or tango dancer, sign up for classes, take lessons, or put in your application for the position. If you're terrified of flying or scuba diving, book a trip and get yourself into the plane or the water. Anytime we have the courage to face a fear directly, even if the results aren't perfect, we will find that our fear decreases and our sense of self grows. "Do the thing you fear, and the death of fear is certain," wrote Ralph Waldo Emerson. Facing our fears helps us grow and leads us closer to a sense of our true Essence.

The fourth option for handling fear is faith. "Faith in yourself and faith in God are the key to mastery of fear," wrote ESP expert and psychic researcher Harold Sherman. Faith teaches us that we can rely on our abilities. Faith reminds us that we have inside us the same Essence that moves the universe and creates miracles both here and in the hereafter. Faith helps us turn and fight or make the changes we need, because faith gives us strength and confidence in ourselves. Faith reminds us that our primary purpose on Earth is to learn and grow, and that anything we fear is part of that journey. Take the energy of fear and turn it to faith. Make it a challenge in your life. As my friend Mark always said, "When the going gets tough, the tough get creative!" In time, we may come to see our fears as guides that show us where our greatest work is to be done, and when we learn to handle them, we are ready for bigger challenges. "The fishermen know that the sea is dangerous and the storm terrible, but they have never found these dangers sufficient reason for remaining ashore," wrote Vincent van Gogh.

Fear also can turn us toward Essence as the last source of strength. Sometimes it takes a strong emotion like fear to get past our barriers and put us on our knees. Fear can help us transcend our own limitations and discover a greater source of love and wisdom. "Fear is the needle that pierces us, that it may carry a thread to bind us to heaven," wrote James Hastings. When we draw our strength from Essence, when we seek for goodness in ourselves and others and work to bring what goodness we can to Earth, we can vanquish our fears while we learn and grow, becoming more like our true nature every day. Then we are truly ready to fight on the side of the angels.

YOUR SOUL'S ENERGY BOOSTERS

- We have choice and free will, which means we are free to choose the path and actions that draw us closer or take us further away from Essence.
- Good and evil seem to be a part of the fabric of the universe. We need duality—both the energy of good and its opposite.
- Goodness has to work ten times harder to win but is always stronger in the long run. To cover a coat of white paint it only takes one coat of black. To cover a coat of black paint, it takes ten coats of white.
- There is always justice and repayment for transgressions and deeds of evil.
- Just as there are good and bad people on Earth, there are positive and negative energies in the spirit world.
- No one on Earth or in spirit, has power over us unless we give it to them.
- We are the hands of good in the battle against evil, so we must be willing to stand up to evil and say no, to challenge evil and stop it from acting in our lives as well as the lives of others.
- We must be willing to stand and fight on the side of the angels and be strong. We have free will and the power to choose good and learn from our poor choices.
- There is good fear and bad fear. Good fear can be a warning that something is wrong. Bad fear blocks you from Essence and your intuition that can warn

you of problems, and it stops you from attaining your goals.

- Faith in yourself and faith in God are the key to mastering fear.
- Fear can also turn us toward Essence as the last source of strength. Sometimes it takes a strong emotion like fear to get past our barriers and put us on our knees. Fear can help us transcend our own limitations and discover a greater source of love and wisdom.
- There is eternal justice that rewards good and punishes evil. We cannot understand this until we pass over to the other side.
- The more good we do and the better we become in this life, the better the neighborhood of energy we will transition to when our physical body dies on the earth.
- We help loved ones in the spirit world by praying for their healing.
- It is important to protect yourself from negative energy using the mirrored egg and the white light.

EIGHT

Love in All Its Glory

Love is a word of light, written by a hand of light, upon a page of light.

—KAHLIL GIBRAN

We are born with the need to give and receive love. If we don't love ourselves and have the opportunity to love others, we wither and die. We're taught in school that the molecules and atoms of our bodies are mostly space in between minute specks of matter; well, I believe that the space in between is composed of the energy of love—it's that necessary to our very existence. "The superiority that has no superior; the redeemer and instructor of souls, as it is their primal essence, is love," wrote Ralph Waldo Emerson. Love arises in every circumstance and for every possible reason. We love some people for their external beauty, others even though they have no beauty at all. (Think of babies—they are loved no matter how wrinkled, fat, or homely they may be. If you ever doubt that beauty does not determine love, look at some of the pets that people lavish their affection upon!) We love some people for their nobility and others in spite of their misdeeds. Love can take the form of admiration and pity, desire and selflessness, acceptance and holding someone to a high standard. Love is infinitely flexible and supremely constant. Love is like a river whose surface is never the same, yet underneath the current flows, strong, silent, powerful, and irresistible. Love is what we are made of and who we are, if we only recognize and acknowledge it. Mahatma Gandhi said, "Love . . . is the law of our Being." Love is essential for life.

Everyone has within them the capacity to love and be loved simply because we are all part of Essence, and Essence is composed of love. When we love, we are connecting with Essence in the other, even if that Essence is hidden. More important, when we love, we connect more fully with the Essence inside ourselves. That's why love is such a divine emotion—because it aligns us with the divinity inside our own hearts. The love we feel is a reflection and reminder of the love that Essence has for each of us. However, love must begin by loving ourselves before we can share love with others. Too many people pursue relationships because they don't love or appreciate themselves and they need another person to make them feel complete. But we must be complete in ourselves first; only then can we relate to others in a healthful way. Love starts with connecting with our own Essence and seeing ourselves as both loving and worthy of love. The first true love is self-love. It doesn't mean you are selfish. It means your needs matter.

The ultimate goal of every relationship is to connect ever

more deeply to our shared Essence. The journey to this goal can be bumpy or smooth. Sometimes it's hard to remember a baby's Essence when it's screaming, or a lover's Essence when they say something cruel, or a friend's Essence when they ignore us—or our own Essence when we do those things ourselves. Relating to others can be difficult, but the lessons we are taught in relationships are probably the most important we will learn on Earth. We learn how easy it is to be hurt or to hurt others. We learn the glories of love and its consolations; the pain of losing love, and the pain of being the one to leave when love changes. With each lesson, we are reminded again and again of the necessity of love in our lives. And if we keep these lessons in mind, then every relationship is an opportunity to grow more and more in Essence.

Love is, above all, the gift of oneself.

—JEAN ANOUILH

Think about the first time you met someone whom you came to love. What was it inside them that called to you? I believe it's because we feel the Essence of the other person. Any relationship is about two people discovering their common Essence. This may be a long process, as in a friendship that develops slowly, or it can be instantaneous, like love at first sight or when a mother looks at her new baby. Our relationships—good or bad, ecstatic or painful, long or short—are the gifts of Essence, designed to help us connect, learn, and grow.

Relationships are the perfect mirror; we learn more about ourselves in our relationships than we ever could learn anywhere else. Relationships put our concepts of who we are to the test. We can believe that we are loving, spiritual beings and then find ourselves exploding when our spouse fails to call, or our kids make a mess, or our parents or friends make an unreasonable demand. On the other hand, we can feel more spiritual when we are sharing love with someone than we might feel after hours of meditation and prayer. Ask a mother who is holding her child or someone ministering to a dying person if they don't feel a true spiritual connection and love in those moments. Relationships are magnifiers: we are better and worse with the people we love than with anyone else. We can see in them the things that drive us crazy about ourselves, as well as the things we would most like to be. Relationships bring out the truth in us and in others. It's harder to lie to ourselves and maintain the façade we may present to the rest of the world, because our loved ones know us too well to let us get away with it for long! I think if you were to ask people to name the one thing that would cause them to leave any relationship, the top of the list would be lying or deliberate deception of any kind. The basis of any lasting relationship entails connecting with the truth of the other person and letting them connect with the truth of who you are.

Relationships require trust, and trust must be based in the faith that the other has your best interests at heart as you have theirs. The Anglican wedding service solemnizes the relationship of marriage as a place in which "each member of the family, in good times and in bad, may find strength, companionship, and comfort, and grow to maturity in love." This describes our responsibility in any relationship: we are mutually responsible for support and love, to bring out the best in the other as they bring out the best in us. When we do so, then our relationships truly become gifts and reflections of Essence.

The First Relationship: Family

The family is the country of the heart.

—GIUSEPPE MAZZINI

The family is the essential relationship and the means of our first lessons on Earth. Our connection to our family is our earliest experience of love, and often our strongest. In most families, parents gladly sacrifice for their children, and children willingly care for their parents as they age. The lessons we learn within our families will shape who we are and how we walk through the world. Indeed, how we interact with our family determines how we experience every kind of love, including the divine. Is it any wonder that so many cultures call divine Essence *Father* or *Mother*?

I was blessed to have wonderful parents. They taught me love, compassion, and humor; they showed me the importance of standing up for myself and doing what's right. Most of all, they were models of loving relationships, both with their three daughters and with each other. Of course, growing up, I didn't always see them as wonderful—no teenager thinks their mother or father knows anything! And I've also seen and heard about the difficulties others have had with their parents. But I firmly believe that when we are incarnated, we choose to be born into certain families and to certain parents. Parents teach us about who we are and what we can expect from life. Ultimately, they are our first teachers of the most important lesson we could learn: the lesson of love.

No matter what karma we bring into this world, every birth is a fresh start. "Every child comes with the message that God is not yet discouraged of man," wrote Rabindranath Tagore. Sometimes when you look into the eyes of a baby or a young child, you can see the wisdom, goodness, and love of Essence shining through. Maybe that's part of the reason we treasure our children, because they remind us of our own inner divinity. Unfortunately, we are not yet at the point where our love is as pure, wise, and unconditional as Essence's love for us, so the love we give our children is all too often flawed. As someone once said, we're all amateur parents, and we pass along to our children the lessons we have learned from our parents, the good and the bad. We choose our parents according to the lessons we are supposed to learn. If our karma was to be born in a family of alcoholics, that will affect how we raise our kids. If our karma was to be born in a family with loving relations, that, too, will shape our children's lives as well as our own. An easy or difficult childhood is not an accident but a result of both the karma we created in past lifetimes and the karma we have lived in this one.

Our primary job as parents is to remember that each child is a unique soul that has been entrusted to us, and we must appreciate that soul's uniqueness and give children the support they need. We do this by *choosing the path of love whenever possible.* We are born from love, and we should live and move in love, because that is our nature. The problem lies when we forget this fact and respond out of frustration, anger, or hurt. Being a parent is probably the most difficult thing we will ever have to do because it is the biggest responsibility we will ever have. Being a child isn't easy either, considering that we often must learn the hard way—by making mistakes, by trying and failing, and certainly by experiencing frustration that we cannot do or be what we want in the moment. But how much easier is our task as parents or children if we remember that our true nature is love! Love looks for commonalities rather than separation; love sees the highest even in the lowest of moments. When we actively seek the most loving choice in the moment, we are teaching our children to use love as the benchmark for their future actions. Proverbs 22:6 reminds us, "Train up a child in the way he should go: and when he is old, he will not depart from it." By doing our best to respond with love, we are helping both our children and ourselves to create more loving families now and in the future.

Of course, that doesn't mean that parents should let their children run wild, or they should condone behaviors like using drugs or alcohol. It also doesn't mean that children should "turn the other cheek" and endure being treated poorly by family members or anyone else. Love can give parents and children the strength to ask to be treated with love and respect. Love can help parents to make the tough decisions to place a child in rehab, or help a child to stand up to an abusive or indifferent parent or teacher. Remember, love must always start with self-love and self-respect. Choosing love often means choosing what will be best for both parent and child, even though the decision is painful in the moment. The key is always to ask, "What would Essence want for both of us?" Remember, our children have chosen us and we have chosen our parents to be our partners this time around. When love is the basis of our family relationship, then we will indeed be training up the child in the way he should go, and we can use the lessons to grow in love as well.

A brother is a friend provided by nature.

—LEGOUVÉ PÉRE

Our siblings often have just as much influence upon us as our parents. Indeed, as someone once commented, because our parents probably will die before us, we will have our relationships with brothers and sisters longer than any other. As I was blessed with my parents, I also have been blessed to have two wonderful older sisters, who were my babysitters, defenders, role models, and guides growing up. There is no better feeling than knowing you have people in this world who will be on your side no matter what, who have known you all of your life and who have shared both the high and low points. I saw this clearly when I read for a woman who had lost her beloved brother. "His name was Joost, but you had a nickname for him—Brocha, Little Brother?" I told her. "He loved you unconditionally, and he says he will always be there for you and for your son." It felt as if Joost were sitting next to me in the room, the energy of his love for his sister was so strong. Brothers and sisters can be our dearest friends and greatest examples of what to do and what to avoid doing. And while our relationships with siblings often change many times over a lifetime, we should treasure them for the gifts they are.

Friends: The Other Family

A friend is a second self.

—ARISTOTLE

Friends are the family we choose while we are here on Earth. Our friends are a direct reflection of who we believe we are and how we see ourselves. And, like our family, the bonds of friendship may be forged on the other side long before we're born. Have you ever had an immediate connection with a stranger, an instant sense of liking and curiosity? Often that stranger becomes your best friend, and you keep track of him or her even if you are separated by time and distance. In such cases, there may be a karmic relationship from a past life. With our friends, we feel we know who they truly are, and we feel their truth resonating with ours. This kind of deep-seated friendship enriches our lives.

Friendships can uplift us and support us in connecting with Essence, or they can encourage us to make choices that take us lower instead of higher. Friends can lead the way or encourage us to turn around and settle for less than who we are or what we can be. Whenever we look at our friendships, we first need to look at ourselves. As friends, we should have each other's best interests at heart. What kind of friends are we? Do we encourage others to be their best, or do we secretly like it when we entice someone else into being bad? Are we helping our friends to learn and grow, or are we holding them back? It can be difficult if we feel our friends growing apart from us because they are changing and we are not (or vice versa). If this occurs, we have two choices. First, if our friends are growing better and wiser, then we need to look at ourselves and see what we need to do to keep up with them. Friends can open doors for us that we might never have opened otherwise. Friends can take us in new directions and keep us company so the way is not as intimidating as it would be if we traveled alone. "Friendship is a strong and habitual inclination in two persons to promote the good and happiness of one another," wrote Eustace Budgell. When our friends challenge us and support us in our growth, and we do the same for them, then friendship becomes a vital part of our journey.

Second, if our friends are heading in the other direction—away from Essence and toward darkness or complacency—we must be good enough friends to challenge them and to uplift them when we can, and if we can't, be willing to leave the relationship. Sometimes people who we think are our good friends are actually *energy vampires*. These can be friends who are always seeking your love and attention to the exclusion of others and with no regard of your needs. Conversely, energy vampires can be friends who let you put all the effort into the relationship. You're there for them when they need you, but if you ask for anything, they've always got a reason why they are not available. Friendship should be a relationship of equals, where both people come to give and receive love. Certainly the equality of friendship is an ever-shifting balance, where one friend gives and the other receives, one friend supports and the other is supported, depending on the circumstances. But if in a friendship the balance is habitually unequal, with one friend being overly needy and the other always giving, or one friend putting their needs first and the other always giving in, then the lesson may be to either change the relationship or to leave it.

All too often, we are tempted by the easy path of maintaining the friendship with our silence even when we know our friends are making bad choices. We justify their actions by saying things like "They're going through a bad patch," "It's just a phase," "It's only one time," or worst of all, "It's not my job to change him—he's just a friend." It could be that your greatest lesson is to be courageous enough to challenge your friend on the choices that are leading toward darkness instead of light. You may need this lesson at a later point in life—when you're faced with the same situation with your child, or grandchild, or yourself. Emerson wrote, "The only way to have a friend is to be one." We must be courageous, loving, and wise enough to challenge ourselves and our friends to do what's right, to continue to grow, and to deepen our relationships, not just with each other but with the Essence that lies within us both. Eventually, we may need to leave the friendship if it doesn't support us. Ending friendships is rarely easy, but as with all our relationships, our only responsibility is to be the best friend possible, send love to those who have touched our lives, and bless them on their way.

For many of us, our pets and other animals are some of our greatest friends. Many of us learn our very first lessons of unconditional love not from our family or friends but from our pets. The love of pets is unconditional and uncomplicated. It teaches us about the power of love to connect us directly to the heart of another—even when that being has four legs, or fur, or hooves, or scales. When you have a pet or animal companion, you can sense their Essence clearly because there's very little to get in the way. And I believe that our pets can sense our Essence as well—which is probably one of the reasons they will put up with us!

In the same way it's really difficult when we lose any loved one, the death of a pet can be very hard on us, whether we're a child or an adult. However, I can say with certainty that our beloved animal friends will be there for us in heaven. Not too long ago, I read for a family whose mother raised champion show dogs. After she passed away, I went to her house, where I immediately could feel the mother's spirit. "She's with Moni, her favorite dog," I reassured the family. I pointed to a photo of the woman surrounded by her champion spaniels. "She's telling me, that one's Moni. Your mom is still taking care of her dogs on the other side, and she's very happy." When you pass to the other side, know that you're likely to see your favorite dog or cat or bird or horse waiting for you, greeting you with affection, ready to brighten your (eternal) life.

The Gifts of Intimate Relationships

There is only one happiness in life, to love and be loved.

—GEORGE SAND

Finding a partner with whom to share love is one of the great experiences of life. We feel an energy that draws us close and makes it seem as if the whole world is lit from the inside. In an intimate relationship, we can feel a sense of newness, freshness, and discovery, and at the same time it can feel so natural to have this person in our lives. We are one being instead of two. As the poet John Milton said of intimate love, "We are . . . One Flesh; to lose thee were to lose my self."

Scientist Masaru Emoto describes love as a kind of resonance frequency. This frequency can be higher or lower depending upon circumstances. Have you ever looked back on intimate relationships you had several years ago and been amazed (or chagrined) at the partners you chose back then? Perhaps it's because today you are resonating at a higher level, and you are attracting partners who possess the same frequency. When we get into an intimate relationship, we find that our "love frequency" shifts into alignment with our partner. If a good girl goes out with a bad boy, for instance, something in each of them has resonated with the other. Either the good girl may sense an essential goodness in the bad boy, or something inside her resonates with his wild rule-breaker energy. However, if they are going to create a relationship, either the bad boy is going to change his wild ways, or the good girl is going to start being bad. In our intimate relationships, we must resonate in tune with our partners. It's like two tuning forks being placed next to each other. One adjusts its frequency to match the note produced when the other is struck; otherwise, there is disharmony.

This tendency of our intimate relationships to lead our energy higher or lower is why we must be careful when it comes to choosing our partners. And that begins by being wise enough to know ourselves intimately before we become intimate with another. When we know ourselves, we are less likely to fall for someone's outward appearance or our childhood dreams of the perfect partner, and more likely to be attracted to someone who resonates with our deepest impulses, our true nature. We spoke earlier about the law of attraction, how our energy and our thoughts can draw events, people, and things to us. When we know ourselves clearly and understand what we want in an intimate partner, it helps us both focus our energy to attract that kind of person and to notice them when they show up. Have you ever heard someone say, "I knew John for years, but one day I saw something in him I'd never seen before"? Or "I bought dozens of books in that bookstore and never noticed Sam, but one day something clicked"? Sometimes we don't realize how special a relationship is until we start to explore the energy between ourselves and the other person. The new feelings and experiences we create together help it to grow.

However, we must be aware if there is anything that is blocking our energy and preventing us from finding a good partner. If we are just leaving a bad relationship, for example, we may end up attracting someone whose inner energy connects with our negative feelings around relationships. Our energy around intimate relationships also can be muddied if our parents had problems with each other, or we were denied the love of either parent. Many times, people do this in romance and attract themselves to the energy of an abusive parent or the parent from whom they never received love or approval. They go into a relationship with someone like this parent and try to "fix" him or her. Unfortunately, they will keep repeating this pattern until they recognize it for what it is. If we're not careful, we can develop a bad habit of choosing partners that are unhealthy for us. We must make ourselves ready to attract love by clearing away any past or present barriers to it. This may mean some kind of counseling, or it could simply be a function of taking a little time off so you can get back in touch with your Essence. When we know that we are made of love, and when we remember that love brings not pain but life, then we will attract the life-affirming relationships that we desire.

However, we also may need to protect our energy when we are seeking to create an intimate relationship. There are dark energies in the world that are attracted to the light so they can diminish it. Sometimes dark energy can masquerade as light, or it can raise its frequency for a short time and draw us in. Whenever you focus on manifesting an intimate relationship, make sure you ask that you attract only the highest energy of light and love. Be willing to look beyond the exterior to the heart and soul of potential partners. We all have pictures of who our ideal intimate partner will be, but we may find the perfect partner in a different form from what we expect. Be clear about the feeling you want to have with your intimate partner, ground that feeling of love in your experience of Essence, and then notice when you have that feeling in the company of another person.

Love is our Essence, and our nature is to express that love. But if we seek love in others because without it we feel incomplete, then we are doomed to failure. No human love can make us "complete," because we are complete already. The love at the core of our being is endless, with no need of another person or object. The words of one of the great lovers in literature, Juliet, describe accurately the love that is Essence: "My bounty is as boundless as the sea, / My love as deep; the more I give to thee, / The more I have, for both are infinite." Any relationship based on needing another to feel whole creates an unhealthy dependence. When an incomplete partner joins another incomplete partner, it can create a habitual battle of whose needs come first. When an incomplete partner joins a complete partner, the inequality of the relationship will cause resentment on one side and fatigue on the other. True intimacy only arises when completeness joins completeness, when we sense the Essence of another person and they sense ours. If you've ever said of an intimate partner, "It seems as if they know my soul," or "I love them for who they are inside," then you probably are sensing their Essence. We feel that we're looking at the real person, not the mask or illusion or façade. We're looking into the eyes of their soul, and they are looking into ours. When both partners are secure in their infinite capacity of love, love expands to encompass them both.

The Truth About Soul Mates

A soul mate is someone who helps your soul to grow.

—CHAR

We've been taught to define soul mates the way Kahlil Gibran defines them: as "my other, beautiful half, which I have lacked ever since we emerged from the sacred hand of God." We think of a soul mate as the part of us that we must seek throughout lifetimes, and without whom we are incomplete. That's a beautiful definition, but it doesn't encompass the true wonder of soul mates or describe their true function. A soul mate incarnates to help us grow. Our soul mate may indeed be our romantic "other half," or they may be our greatest adversary. We have met our soul mates in many lifetimes, in many different forms. How our soul mate incarnates depends upon the lesson we need to learn this time around.

When someone comes for a reading and asks, "Will I meet my soul mate?" it tends to raise a flag of caution with me. We may have someone we're destined to meet, even destined to be with; on the other hand, what if our destiny is to learn to recognize love in other forms? What if our soul mate is our child, or brother, or parent?

What if our soul mate's job is to teach us about jealousy, obsession, or the pain of loss? Wishing for a soul mate can be dangerous, because you never know what lessons our soul mate has to teach. Ask for the qualities you want in someone but never a specific person. There is an old saying, "*Be careful what you ask for, you may get it.*"

Looking for a soul mate also can keep us from seeing other opportunities for love. Sometimes we close ourselves off to the love Essence is offering us in our quest for the ideal version of the perfect mate. Remember, love appears in many guises and grows at many different speeds. If you're waiting for lightning bolts and angelic choirs to let you know your soul mate has arrived, you're liable to spend your life waiting and looking in vain. Occasionally, we are fated to have the "flash of lightning" explosion of mutual love, but in many lifetimes, we connect with our soul mates gently, over the years, and we may recognize them as our soul mates only when we meet them on the other side. I also believe there can be more than one soul mate for each of us, because our souls need different things at different times. Your next (or current) partner may or may not be your soul mate, but they will serve some universal purpose in your life. Love has too many gifts to be confined to one particular form, package, or expectation.

Relationships are some of our greatest joys and greatest teachers and are among the primary ways our karma plays itself out. While I believe we create a lot of our own destiny in our relationships, I've also encountered many relationships that seemed to be predestined. Perhaps the person you meet in grade school that becomes your best friend was your spouse in another lifetime, or the boss who is such a taskmaster was the servant you treated poorly the last time around. If you've ever felt a strong connection with someone and had no explanation for it, often it's because destiny and karma are involved, and there has to be some kind of balancing and healing for both of you to grow and move on. I also think sometimes that relationships end when our karma with this person is complete. A friend of a friend was married for twenty years and then found himself irresistibly attracted to another woman. He was still in love with his wife, but he felt compelled to leave her for his new girlfriend. He said to his wife, "I know this is painful, but I think this is happening because you're supposed to do something great, and you would never step out on your own if we stayed together." He was right. Within two years, the wife had written a bestselling book and became a sought-after teacher and seminar leader. Both spouses have remarried and are very happy with their new partners. They had worked through their karma with each other and moved on.

The place we will truly know our soul mates is where we see their souls face-to-face—that is, on the other side. When we pass over, we will see clearly the role our soul mates have played in this lifetime and in lifetimes past, and we will appreciate fully the gift they have been to us. And we will touch more directly the Essence that we share with our soul mates and the rest of our friends and family. Perhaps we will even see that in truth, all beings that seek to grow in goodness, wisdom, and love are our soul mates.

Sharing Our Deepest Nature with Others

My heart will be your shelter, and my arms your home.

—WEDDING VOWS

The word *intimate* is the perfect description of the kind of relationship where we share ourselves fully. But we have to be willing to put in the work to keep the relationship fresh and alive. We must recognize that relationships change as the partners grow and evolve. An intimate relationship of one year's duration will be different from that of a couple celebrating their golden anniversary. It's very easy to get caught up in the drama of what changes and forget the unchangeable core of love that we share with our intimate partner. We must come back to that core again and again if our relationship is to last. We must continually remind each other of who we are and what we share—the Essence of love that draws us together. Often it's the smallest things that help us remember these truths. I know of one couple that exchanges love notes every day. Other couples say, "I love you," before they go to sleep and make it a point never to go to bed angry. A couple I know that travels for business calls or texts each other at least once a day, every day, no matter where they are in the world. Another way to keep relationships fresh is to be each other's champion and pep squad. It's a great feeling to know there's someone in your corner, a person who will cheer you on when you undertake something important. Shared goals in a relationship are also valuable reminders that we are there to support each other's efforts. "Life has taught us that love does not consist in gazing at each other but in looking outward together in the same direction," wrote Antoine de Saint-Exupéry. However, having some separate interests can strengthen a relationship as well. In the same way that we must come into a relationship as a complete human rather than someone who needs another to be whole, separate interests can ensure that we continually bring fresh ideas and perspectives that will expand our partner while enriching the relationship.

Our intimate relationships are the source of our greatest joys and our greatest lessons. Our intimate partner can hurt us more deeply than anyone else. Pain is an inevitable part of every relationship. "The one who loves you will make you weep," according to an Argentine proverb. On Earth, we are human beings with a divine core but limited perceptions. Whether we intend to or not, we will cause pain in our partner, and they will hurt us in turn. A part of being in a relationship is to learn to accept our own limitations as well as the limitations of our partners, and to love them and ourselves in spite of them. Thomas Merton wrote, "I cannot discover God in myself and myself in Him unless I have the courage to face myself exactly as I am, with all my limitations, and to accept others as they are, with all *their* limitations." This is probably one of the most important lessons we will learn in our intimate relationships, because it brings us closer to God.

Quite honestly, feeling pain often isn't the real problem in a relationship, but holding on to pain is. Eckhart Tolle tells a wonderful story about a duck pond. When ducks swim in a pond, sometimes one duck intrudes on another's space and they will start to fight. There's a flurry of wings and beaks, and then it's over. The ducks go back to swimming around the pond as if nothing happened. But if the ducks were like humans, after the fight, one duck would be off in a corner brooding while the other would swim over to its friends to rehash the fight and get angry and hurt all over again! In our intimate relationships, we need to be more duck-like. We need to stand up for what we consider worth fighting for, of course, but we also need to be willing to let go of the residue of a fight. We must practice forgiveness for ourselves and for others. We need to remember the true Essence of our partner and do what we must to appreciate them once more.

Over the years, our connection to a partner can get stronger and stronger as we learn and grow together. True intimacy only gets deeper the more we know and love our partners, especially when we are willing to give them the space to learn and grow and they give us the same. The love we share at eighty will not be the same as it was when we were twenty, but like Essence, its core can remain vibrant, ever new and yet eternal. Like the river, the surface of love may look different from moment to moment, but in its depths, in its most intimate connections, it is always and forever the same.

When Love Changes: Dealing with Loss

No love, no friendship can cross the path of our destiny without leaving some mark on it forever.

—FRANÇOIS MAURIAC

Love never dies, as I've said many times before; but love does change form. Our primary reason for being on Earth is to learn and grow, and both learning and growing mean that we and our circumstances will change. We relate differently to our parents and siblings when we are infants than we do as children living at home, or as adults with families of our own. As we change, we choose different friends, perhaps even different intimate partners. Even if we keep the same friends or partners, our relationships evolve through time, and sometimes that evolution means the transformation or even the loss of the relationship itself. All of this is in preparation for the greatest transformation of all—when we pass to the other side.

Human beings can find it difficult to acknowledge when they are outgrowing a particular relationship or need it to change. That's one of the reasons people stay in abusive families, or loveless marriages, or stick with friends with whom they may no longer have anything in common. But sometimes choosing love necessitates that we leave an old love behind. It's never easy to admit that this person whom we have loved no longer meets our needs. It's even more difficult to come to the realization that we fell in love with an image rather than reality, or that someone has changed in such a way that the relationship no longer supports either party. Dealing with changes in relationships takes honesty, courage, and above all, the kind of love that is willing to admit the truth and do what is best for everyone.

No loss is ever easy, and it's inevitable that we will feel pain and sorrow with the loss of a relationship, no matter how it ends. However, sometimes our greatest gifts can come from the loss of a relationship. It can teach us lessons of humility and compassion. The pain and sadness we feel at the end of a relationship can open us up and make us more vulnerable. The loss can put us in touch with our emotions and with what is truly important. How many of us take the people in our lives for granted day after day, year after year, only to discover when they are gone how deeply we loved them? When we lose someone we love, we value our remaining relationships even more. However, we must never let the loss of a relationship prevent us from loving again. We must always remember that relationships are our gifts from Essence, designed to teach us about giving and receiving, about selflessness and wholeness, and above all, about love.

MOVING ON FROM THE END OF A RELATIONSHIP

When faced with a loss of love, try the following process to help you move through your pain. You may want to write down your answers. At the very least, take some time by yourself to go through each step.

1. ACKNOWLEDGE WHAT'S LOST. Sometimes we try to gloss over our hurt and pretend everything's fine. Even if you were the one to leave, or if you left an abusive relationship, you need to recognize that something is gone. Allow yourself to mourn what is no more, even if it's only the dreams you had when you began the relationship.

2. UNDERSTAND THE LESSONS. The faster we can understand the lessons we were meant to learn, the easier it will be to move forward. What did this relationship teach you about yourself? About love? About what you need in a relationship? About what you won't stand for? What gifts did this relationship bring to you?

3. SAY GOODBYE. Sometimes when we leave a relationship, we feel we have said everything we needed—but more often there is much left unexpressed. Close your eyes and bring the image of the other person to mind. Imagine them sitting in a chair opposite you and say whatever you want to say. If you need to express hurt, anger, upset, frustration, confusion, or any other negative emotion, do so fully. Imagine the other person simply sitting and listening. Keep talking until you've said everything you need to, and see

the other person taking it in completely. Now, share with this person the lessons you discovered in #2. What did he or she teach you? How did you grow? What will be different in your future relationships? Once you've said all this, say goodbye and watch the image of this person stand up and walk out of your life.

4. CREATE THE SPACE FOR A NEW RELATIONSHIP. Get in touch with Essence, the love that is at your core. Feel that love with you, this moment and always. Know that it has been there with you throughout your old relationship, and it will be with you in your new relationship as well. Ask Essence to clear any energy blocks that could get in the way of attracting someone new. Then open your eyes and write down what you wish to find in a new relationship. Make sure your list includes not only what you want in this other person but also what you *don't* want. Just as important, make sure you write what you are committed to *giving* in this new relationship. Then, with clear energy and a specific focus, watch to see what Essence will bring into your life.

Relationships are a path to growth as well as love. We must not be too sad when a relationship ends; instead, we should cherish the fact that this person shared our lives, if only for a moment, and gave us an opportunity to share our Essence with them. We must regard each parting as a rehearsal for the greatest transformation of all: when our spirits pass from this side into eternity.

It is love, not reason, that is stronger than death.

—THOMAS MANN

As a child, did you ever make a "telephone" from two paper cups and a piece of string? You put a hole in the bottom of the cups and thread the string through the holes, connecting the cups like old-fashioned telephones. If you stretch the string taut and speak into one paper cup while someone else holds the other paper cup to their ear, you can hear what's being said; the sound travels along the string between the cups. Love is like that string. It's as if there is a golden thread spanning from the Essence inside of us to the Essence inside the person we love. The thread may be invisible and it may stretch to the breaking point, but as long as we care for the other, the thread will not break. Love is the link between us and those we love, and it does not vanish after death. As I've said time and again, love is our strongest connection with those on the other side. Whenever we think loving thoughts of a departed partner, spouse, child, parent, or friend, love transmits our thoughts past any barrier, including the barrier of death.

One of the sweetest readings I've done in a long time was for Cindy and her fiancé, Peter. Cindy wanted to know if her father, who had died several years earlier, approved of Peter. The first thing her dad gave me was the name Jonah. "That's my son," Peter said. "He's going to be walking down the aisle with Cindy when we get married."

"Usually, the father walks the bride down the aisle, but Jonah's doing it," I told them. "Your dad is saying that he's happy about that, and he's going to be at your wedding in spirit. Now he's crying—he says you'll always be his little girl, Cindy. He's handing you a flower, a single flower. Is there a special single flower in your bouquet?"

Peter looked at me. "I picked out Cindy's bouquet, and yes, there's one different flower in it. It's a surprise. How did you know?"

I smiled. "Cindy's father is saying that the special flower is from him. He really likes you, Peter." It was one of the nicest blessings a father could have given his family on Earth.

We are made of love, born of love, live in love, and carry love with us when we pass to the other side. Indeed, love is the only thing that we take with us. Love never dies, and the love we share with those on Earth will continue throughout eternity. This can be hard to remember when we are faced with the loss of a loved one. Death can bring out the worst and best in us, can cause us to remember our love for the person that's gone with pain, because they are no longer here in physical form. Death also can remind us of our own mortality and bring up fear, which can block our experience of love.

It's important for us to recognize both the fact and the reality of death. The fact of death is that our loved ones are no longer in physical form; we will miss their touch and their loving presence. However, what we truly love about our dear ones will never die. At the moment of physical death, the Essence of this person will pass from this world to the next, changing form but not its deepest nature. Love links Essence to Essence, and Essence is eternal. What we love is not simply the temporary shell of a person, or the amalgamation of experience that has made up a life, or the personality traits that have helped to endear this person to us. When we love, we love the soul of a person. Who we are at our core connects with the core of another, the part of them that is eternal.

When you love, you should not say, "God is in my heart," but rather, "I am in the heart of God."

—KAHLIL GIBRAN

The ultimate goal of any earthly relationship is to reflect and remind us of our deepest relationship: that with Essence. "As above, so below; as below, so above," someone wrote. "Love your Heavenly Father as I have loved you," said Jesus. "God is Love, Love is God, you are loved, we love you," my father wrote in my prayer book. Loss of an outer focus of our love can lead us to a greater recognition of the only inner source of love that is unchanging: the God inside our hearts who teaches us again and again about the undying, eternal glory of love. That is the real reason for, and the ultimate glory of, relationships. It is why they are our greatest treasure, both here and in heaven.

YOUR SOUL'S ENERGY BOOSTERS

- We are born with the need to give and receive love. If we don't love ourselves and have the opportunity to love others, we wither and die.
- God is Love; Love is God. Essence is composed of love.
- Relationships are the perfect mirror. We learn more about ourselves in our relationships than we ever could learn anywhere else.
- Family is the essential relationship and the means of our first lessons on Earth.
- We choose to be born in certain families and to certain parents.

- An easy or difficult childhood is not an accident but a result of both the karma we created in past lifetimes and the karma we have lived in this one.
- Friends are the family we choose while we are on Earth. Friendship should be a relationship of equals, where both come to give and receive love.
- Many of us learn our first lessons of unconditional love not from our family and friends but from our pets. We are reunited with our beloved pets in heaven.
- Self-love comes first. We must be wise enough to know ourselves intimately before we become intimate with another.
- A soul mate is someone who helps your soul to grow.
- Relationships are some of our greatest joys and greatest teachers and are among the primary ways our karma plays itself out.
- No loss is ever easy, and it's inevitable that we will feel pain and sorrow with the loss of a relationship, no matter how it ends.
- Relationships are our gifts from Essence, designed to teach us about giving and receiving, about selflessness and wholeness, and above all, about love.
- Love never dies, as I've said many times before; but love does change form.
- The first true love is self-love. It doesn't mean you are selfish. It means your needs matter.

NINE

Dealing with Change

Change is the law of life.

—JOHN F. KENNEDY

A Sufi master once told the story of a bird that lived in the branches of a dead tree in the middle of the desert. The bird managed to survive by eating the few bugs that it could find in the vicinity of its shelter. One day, a sandstorm howled through the desert and blew down the tree, and the bird was forced to seek shelter elsewhere. It flew for days, with only the hot desert sands beneath it. Finally, it spotted a dark patch on the horizon. With its last bit of strength, the bird flew the remaining miles and came to rest in a beautiful grove of trees filled with fruit. Without the sandstorm and the loss of its former home, the bird would never have found the abundance in which it would now reside.

Sometimes it can feel as if change is like a sandstorm, roaring out of the desert without warning and driving us far from the security of what we have always known. But the truth is that whether change is gradual, like the growth of a child, or sudden, like a sandstorm, it is the only certainty of life. Almost 2,500 years ago, the philosopher Heraclitus wrote, "You cannot step twice into the same river, for other waters are continually flowing on." Change is built into the DNA of the universe. Scientists tell us that the matter and energy that make up everything are in a constant state of change. The cells and organs of our bodies are born and die in a continual cycle of destruction and renewal. Given all of these truths, it's clear that, while the nature of Essence is eternal and unchanging, it also encompasses constant change and growth within it. As Krishna (an incarnation of Essence) states in the Bhagavad Gita, "I am the origin and the dissolution, the receptacle, the storehouse, and the eternal seed. I now draw in and now let forth; I am death and immortality; I am the cause unseen and the visible effect." Everything changes; nothing is destroyed. Reality is as changeable as the waves of the ocean and as eternal as the ocean itself.

Change presents us with both opportunities and challenges. The changes we want, the ones we believe will have a positive impact, can feel exciting and expansive. Can you remember what it was like to start school, or begin a new relationship or a new job, or move into a new home, or travel to a new city or country? Those positive changes bring a freshness and renewal to our lives. However, in many other circumstances, we can discover the pain of change as well. Losing a friend, a job, a loved one; being turned down for a promotion; a physical condition that hampers your ability to accomplish what you desire. It can be difficult to remember the fundamentally unchanging energy of Essence when we are faced with difficult or painful changes in our lives. Yet it is in the lessons of Essence that we can understand our relationship with change in the most constructive light.

I believe there are some basic truths about change that can help us use it to our advantage. First, *change is a requirement for growth.* Have you ever seen a butterfly struggling to emerge from its cocoon? It's hard work. The butterfly must force its way out, and it can take a long time. But that's what the butterfly needs to do to be strong enough to survive. Once a kindly man saw a butterfly that was stuck halfway out of its cocoon, and so, very gently, he blew on the cocoon, using the warmth of his breath to speed up the process. To his dismay, what finally emerged was a butterfly with stunted wings. Sometimes we need the struggle and effort of change to develop fully. We cannot hurry the process; we can only keep trying to change from what we were to what we wish to become.

Second, *change comes into our lives to teach us valuable lessons.* The core directive of our existence is to learn and grow, and that requires that we change. Sometimes we initiate the changes ourselves; at other times, change comes to us and we are forced to choose new paths and new directions. Every change brings with it the choice either to move further along the path toward Essence, the path of learning and growth, or in the opposite direction, away from Essence, toward stagnation and a decrease in ability and influence. One of our most important lessons is to learn to choose what will help us to continue to evolve ever higher.

> The important thing is this: to be able at any moment to sacrifice what we are for what we could become.
>
> —CHARLES DUBOIS

WHAT CHANGES HAVE YOU MADE ALREADY?

Think about the times when you were faced with a decision to change something of significance: a job, a relationship, a belief. Did you choose to change or stay where you were? What were the results in your life of that decision? Do you feel it expanded your sense of self as it helped you to learn and grow? Or did the decision make you smaller, less capable, more afraid, less open to growth?

We don't have to take every opportunity to change what we're doing, but if we wish to learn and grow, we must always evaluate our opportunities for change by looking at them through the eyes of Essence rather than the eyes of our fear and inertia. When you are faced with change, ask yourself, *What would Essence want of me? Will this change help me to learn and grow closer to my own inner nature?* Then make your choice with courage, knowing that Essence is with you all the way.

The third truth is that *every change has the potential to create ripples far beyond ourselves and this lifetime.* Our choices can change our destiny here on Earth while they create karma that affects our next lifetime. The ripples caused by the changes we make also extend beyond our own lives and into the lives of others. Think of great leaders like Jesus, Buddha, Muhammad, and contemporary figures like Nelson Mandela and Mother Teresa. Each began life as one person with an idea, a vision, a divine inspiration, or a mission. They inspired others to change their ideas and actions to come into alignment with a new way. Eventually, the change they created reached a critical mass and spread far beyond the original source of the vision, idea, or mission. Their ideas and actions changed the world around them, and they continue to inspire us today with their example. When we change, grow, and evolve, we are part of the upliftment of the world.

Fourth, and most important, whenever we are faced with change, *Essence will be there to support us every step of the way.* Because it often entails leaving the familiar behind and going into something new and strange, change can sometimes feel lonely and intimidating. Even when the change is positive—the arrival of a baby, moving to a new city, starting a new class—we can use a supportive "friend" in our corner. Luckily, our friend Essence is with us always. Its love is unchanging, and we can rely upon its goodness and wisdom. We must open ourselves to its presence and seek its guidance for the choices and changes of our lives.

Essence also can help us deal with the two great enemies of change: fear and inertia. When faced with change, it's natural to feel some fear, especially if the change will take us into unknown territory—deciding to get married when we've never been married before, or to have our first child; leaving one career for another; going back to school, or being the first in our family to attend university, and so on. If we can recognize that fear is a natural response to change, then we stand a better chance of controlling our fear and changing instead of letting our fears control us and staying as we are. However, the worst enemy of change isn't fear but inertia. Isaac Newton's first law of motion teaches us that bodies in motion tend to stay in motion, and bodies at rest tend to stay at rest. It takes a lot more effort to get a body at rest to move than it does to keep it moving. We're exactly the same way; it's much harder to take the first step in changing than any other subsequent action. It's much easier to stay in our comfort zone, to play small, and to let opportunities pass us by while we stay right where we are. But that goes against everything that Essence wants for us. We have to be strong enough, courageous enough, to push against inertia and fear and to choose change. When we do, we will be living as Essence wishes us to live.

Change from the Eternal Perspective

What the caterpillar calls the end of the world,
the master calls a butterfly.

—RICHARD BACH

All too often, we judge the events in our lives prematurely, deciding immediately or quickly whether something is "good" or "bad." But months or years later, we understand that something we thought was terrible changed our lives for the better, and the events we thought were spectacular created more difficulties than we would have imagined. We get turned down for a job or a promotion, and it encourages us to start a business that becomes our life's work. We have a health scare that forces us to quit smoking and thus adds years to our lives. One of our children gets arrested for drunk driving or drugs, and the experience completely turns them around. Conversely, we marry the man or woman of our dreams, but within a few years we are walking out the door swearing off relationships for life because of the pain we have experienced. Or the dream job we are offered requires us to work so hard that our health and relationships suffer. Or the beautiful house we buy ends up costing us a fortune in upkeep. To judge something good or bad in the short term is foolish, because the forces of karma and destiny are always at play, and we cannot know the ultimate outcome of our choices.

There's a story about a farmer who lived near a small village. One day, the farmer's only horse ran away. His neighbors said, "That's so terrible. What bad luck!" to which the farmer replied, "Perhaps."

The next morning, the horse returned with three other wild horses. Now the farmer had four horses instead of one!

"You are so lucky," the neighbors told the farmer enviously.

"Perhaps," said the farmer with a shrug. Later that day, the farmer's only son tried to ride one of the wild horses. He was thrown and broke his leg. The son was the farmer's right hand, and he would be unable to work for many weeks.

The neighbors commiserated, "What will you do now? You will lose your farm."

"Perhaps," said the farmer again.

The following week, war was declared, and soldiers swept down on the village, taking every man of military age to go and fight. When they came to the farm, they saw the young man's leg was broken, so they left him behind.

As the neighbors watched their sons march off to fight and die, they cried to the farmer, "You are the most fortunate of us all!"

"Perhaps," said the farmer sympathetically, and turned and went back inside his house.

Joseph Addison wrote, "Our real blessings often appear to us in the shape of pains, losses, and disappointments; but let us have patience, and we soon shall see them in their proper figures." One of the eternal lessons of change is to find our equilibrium no matter what comes into our lives, and to search for the good whenever possible, even when it is very tough to do so. I once read for a couple whose beloved daughter had been killed in an auto accident, and they told me that their daughter's kidneys had been donated to two people who had been waiting six to eight years for transplants. "She's very happy in heaven that she was able to save two lives, and she wants me to thank you for doing that for her. It means a lot to her that you made something so good come out of her passing," I told them. The changes in our lives can be happy or painful, but I believe that if we search for it, there is always some benefit that can be found from Essence's point of view. Even when someone loses a child, or there are terrible events like natural disasters or terrorist bombings, Essence wants us to do whatever we can to create good, even from the worst circumstances. With Essence's support and guidance, it is possible to find the blessing in our challenges. If we seek to create good from evil, we are walking the path of Essence, the path of light that will lead us and others higher.

Essence's Guidance in Times of Change

The capacity for reformation and change lies within.

—PRESTON BRADLEY

In our moments of change and choice, intuition can function as part of our guidance system. Remember, intuition is a direct line to Essence: either Essence can use it to speak to us without our asking, or we can tap into our intuitive sense to ask Essence about the best action to take. Intuition can also put us in touch with the currents of destiny that are flowing through the universe, so we can sense whether this particular change is one that we should make. "All of us have a voice inside that will speak to us if we let it.

Sometimes it's easy to hear; sometimes we have to turn down the volume of the distracting noise around us so we can listen. That voice tells us if we are on the right track," actor Christopher Reeve wrote.

In chapter 3, you learned a way of connecting with Essence using your intuition, and you also learned about the importance of using common sense and logic when making important decisions or dealing with changes. Whenever you're faced with a change in life, whether small or large, try the following.

First, *take a deep breath.* When faced with a situation that may need a change, our first impulse is a reaction rather than a response. We automatically go into an emotional state that shuts down many of the channels of wisdom available to us. Joy over the changes we want, unhappiness over the changes we don't, and excitement and anticipation, or uncertainty and fear, about change in general—emotions such as these can block our awareness of the still, small voice that Essence uses to guide us.

Reactions based on instinct and intuition can be a valuable tool in emergencies, of course. But what about the changes and choices that would benefit from a more considered response? Say your partner walks in one day and announces they are leaving, or you have a big argument and you're the one who impulsively says, "I want a divorce." Sometimes the most difficult thing we can do when faced with change is to slow down and focus; yet often that's a vital first step. Unless you are in a life-or-death situation where you need to make an instant decision, take a deep breath and settle down. You'll be more prepared to deal with change when you can bring *all* your resources to bear. You also may find it easier to listen to the subtle voice of intuition, which often speaks only when our mind and emotions are calm.

Second, *ask for guidance from Essence.* When you are faced with a complicated or difficult choice or change, turning toward the ultimate source of goodness, wisdom, and love and asking for its guidance can help you find your way. Suppose you've been fired from your current job and you decide to go back to school, but you're worried about supporting yourself until you get your degree. Then you get a call from a rival company offering you a position that will entail moving across the country, away from your friends and family. You're faced with some tough decisions: School or work? Stay or move? Take a deep breath, allow your emotions to calm down, and then ask Essence for guidance in making your choice. Believe that Essence wants the best for you and whatever you choose will ultimately be for your highest good.

Third, *bring the powers of logic, common sense, and intuition to bear.* Once your thoughts and emotions are settled and you've asked for guidance, you may find an overwhelming feeling of knowing will awaken inside you and an answer may appear. For example, when you think about that new job offer, maybe it just doesn't feel right. The thought comes up, *I can't be that far away from my family, not now.* This seems strange, as everything is fine with your family, but perhaps two months later, your dad has a heart attack and you need to spend time with him. On the other hand, you may think of going back to school and feel excitement and a sense of expansion. After you've checked your first intuitive impulse, allow your logic and common sense to evaluate the change. What benefits would you receive from the new job or from going back to school? What resources will you need if you were to take the job? How would you support yourself if you went back to school? What effect would your decision have on your friends and family? What impact would each choice have upon your life in both the short and long term? Essence can speak to us not only through our intuition but also through our ability to reason and evaluate.

Fourth, *sleep on your choice if at all possible.* Let the input of intuition, Essence, logic, and common sense "brew," at least overnight. Imagine how you will feel if you take the job, what your life will be like, how the change will shape your future. Then imagine your life back at school. What changes will that create in the years to come? When you take the time to allow all the different kinds of wisdom to integrate in your unconscious and then utilize the power of your imagination to visualize the effects of change in your life, you'll be better prepared to make your choice and feel good about it. Many times, the answer of intuition is an all-knowing feeling; you just know the choice belongs there. You can also consult with friends, family, colleagues you trust. Sometimes Essence can speak most clearly through people we know, who give us a different perspective on our choice without any of the emotional baggage that might be getting in the way of our own inner voice, or who help us interpret the information we're receiving intuitively. Ultimately, however, it will be your choice, so make sure to evaluate any input you receive carefully.

Fifth, *choose the change that fits the best and trust that it is what Essence wants for you.* You must believe that you are making the best choice possible and that you can handle any obstacles or difficulties that come your way. Even though it's natural every now and then to think about the road not taken, the worst thing you can do is to choose and then doubt. Keep checking with your intuition, and always seek to know what Essence's guidance is for your life, but have faith that your chosen course of change is part of the universal plan that will help you learn and grow.

> The more and more each is impelled by that which is intuitive, or the relying upon the soul force within, the greater, the farther, the deeper, the broader, the more constructive may be the result.
>
> —EDGAR CAYCE

Making changes and choosing one good over another (or the lesser of two evils) is rarely easy. To partner with Essence in making change in our lives, we need what I describe as *the four Cs:*

1. COURAGE. As playwright Tennessee Williams describes it, "There is a time for departure even when there's no certain place to go." It takes courage to shape your life not merely based on your own desires or short-term thinking but instead to seek to discover the greater plan and to take action based on faith in yourself and in the guiding hand of Essence. We must have the courage to leave the known and strike out into the unknown.

2. CONFIDENCE. You need confidence both in your choices and, more important, in your ability to handle whatever arises as the result of your choices. You also must have confidence that Essence has only your best interests at heart. "There's a divinity that shapes our ends / Rough-hew them how we will," Shakespeare wrote. You are never alone when you choose to make a change; Essence is always there to take care of you no matter what the outcome.

3. COMMITMENT. Courage and confidence will get you started, but commitment will keep you going through the

toughest times. Change requires that you choose your new path again and again. You can choose to exercise, for instance, but for any real physical benefit you will need to commit to exercising regularly. "Great works are performed not by strength but by perseverance," wrote Samuel Johnson. The great work of change requires your commitment to stick with what you have started. Your intuitive ability is like a muscle; the more you use it, the stronger it gets.

4. CONQUER. Learning and growing require you to conquer both the inner and outer obstacles that try to impede your progress. You must overcome any tendency to look back and say, "If only . . . ," or to give up when the road gets difficult. You must also conquer rigidity in yourself. One of your greatest lessons may be flexibility, to change your approach or even to admit the choice you made didn't pan out. Continue to listen closely to the inner voice of Essence, follow its guidance as well as the guidance of common sense and logic, and you will finish your life as a victor. When you get an intuitive feeling of guidance, be brave and most of all act upon it.

Coping with Unexpected Challenges

God always has another custard pie up his sleeve.

—LYNN REDGRAVE

Sometimes we get a chance to prepare ourselves for a change. We graduate from a university and get our first job. We move in with our boyfriend or girlfriend, and/or we get married. We have a child, or our last child leaves home. We leave a company, or we retire from working altogether. We can close one door with confidence, knowing clearly which door we will open next. But what about the challenges that slap us in the face? The accident on our drive to school or work. Getting laid off or fired. The sudden promotion or job change or transfer to another city. An unexpected pregnancy or miscarriage. Losing money in what you thought was a sure investment. A doctor saying "Your leg is broken" to a competitive athlete, or "Your child is autistic" to a parent, or "You have cancer" to anyone. In life, we are guaranteed to go through unexpected changes that tax our strength and test our will. In some cases, they demand we change; in others, they demand we try harder. In all cases, they can serve as vehicles to draw us closer to the strength of Essence that lies within us all. When people suffer through horrific circumstances, they suddenly recognize what truly is important and who they really are, and identify their purpose on Earth. "Do not pray for easier lives. Pray to be stronger men," said John F. Kennedy. The challenges we undergo can connect us more closely to Essence than easier lives ever would.

It's also important to remember that our challenges may simply be roadblocks that are telling us to slow down and perhaps take another road. Suppose you want to attend a particular school or you want a certain job. You do everything you can to reach your goal, but all of a sudden something gets in your way. You get into the school, but you don't have the money to pay for it. You are called in for a second interview for the job, only to have your boss pull you aside and tell you that she happens to know the top candidate is someone else. In each of these circumstances, you've hit a roadblock, and you need to decide what your next step will be. Do you change your goal, or take action to surmount the block? The more important question is, what choice will bring you the greatest growth? And what will be in alignment with your inner sense of what Essence desires for you? It's far too easy in our goal-oriented, change-driven world to forget that ultimately everything flows according to a universal plan. Even our biggest challenges are part of the great design, and if we're smart, we do our best to align ourselves with the plan rather than fighting it. Suppose you don't have enough money for school; what does Essence tell you? Should you attend a different school that costs less? Perhaps you'll meet your soul mate at that school, someone you never would have found otherwise. Should you work for a year and save your money and then go to school? Maybe the work experience will point you toward an entirely different career, one in which you are destined to make your mark. Should you apply for grants, loans, and scholarships until you have the funds to pay for school? Your lesson in this case could be to keep going even in the face of roadblocks. The best way to deal with challenges, unexpected or otherwise, is to regard them as both an opportunity for growth and a chance to discover the path that Essence wishes us to walk.

Sometimes the biggest lessons of unexpected challenges are trust and faith. We can't know everything that Essence has in store for us, and we can't really know the lessons we are meant to learn until we see our lives as a whole. We must trust that, if we do the best we can, the outcome will be as Essence directs. And we must have faith, a belief that we are guided. Everyone is fated to go through challenges, but the course of our lives will be determined less by *what* we face and more by *how* we face it. The secret is to be ready, keep connected with Essence, trust, and have faith that we are loved and will be cared for. In 1963 in the United States, in the midst of the civil rights struggle, a church in Birmingham was firebombed, and four young girls who were attending Sunday school were killed.

The Reverend Martin Luther King, Jr. spoke eloquently at their memorial service about the pain of facing such a seemingly senseless and insurmountable challenge. His words remind us and inspire us today of the power of Essence to support us in our times of trouble.

> *Life is hard, at times as hard as crucible steel. It has its bleak and difficult moments. Like the ever-flowing waters of the river, life has its moments of drought and its moments of flood. Like the ever-changing cycle of the seasons, life has the soothing warmth of its summers and the piercing chill of its winters. But if one will hold on, he will discover that God walks with him, and that God is able to lift you from the fatigue of despair to the buoyancy of hope and transform dark and desolate valleys into sunlit paths of inner peace.*

In moments of crisis or pain, remember that no matter what happens, we can connect to Essence simply by asking for its help. We must be ready for whatever change may come our way, and if the change is hard to bear, know that Essence will always be there, lifting us up from despair and toward the light of hope.

Change and Acceptance of What Is

God, grant me the serenity to accept the things I cannot change, the courage to change the things I can, and the wisdom to know the difference.

—REINHOLD NIEBUHR

Change and choice operate in the greater framework of Essence, karma, and destiny. We can try to change something in our lives by making a new choice, but karma still must come into play. Suppose you just discovered that your spouse is having an affair. You still love your spouse and don't want to leave the marriage, so you ask him or her to break off the other relationship. You also decide to take responsibility for making your relationship better by being more loving and more attentive to your partner. You change yourself to be a better spouse. However, you have karma with your spouse based on a relationship in a past life where you left them. No matter how many changes you make, your karma in this life is to be deserted, just as you were the one to leave the last time around. So your partner leaves and you feel the pain of losing the relationship. What you did at one time you now must suffer. That's the real purpose of karma; it's not revenge or evening the score as much as it is a means for Essence to make us feel the impact of our deeds on others' lives by making us experience the same in our own.

Sometimes the most painful lesson we can learn is that certain things are not meant to be. We can give it our best shot, change everything about ourselves, be persistent, pray to our higher power that connects us to Essence, and so on, but we still don't reach the result we desire. In every race, there is someone who finishes first, and then there's the rest of the field. Those who focus only on finishing first can sometimes miss the real lesson of the race: who we become in the pursuit of our goal. If your spouse ends the relationship despite all your efforts, it is natural to mourn the loss. But once you have given yourself time to heal, take a look at how much better a lover you will be the next time. What lessons did you learn about showing love to someone else? Will you be more sensitive to others' feelings? Will you be clearer and stronger when it comes to stating your needs up front to a partner, and understanding what they need in a relationship before you make a commitment? (I know of one couple that sat together on their first date and told each other exactly what they wanted in a relationship. They've been married now for more than ten years and make it a point to review their lists every year to make sure each partner knows what the other wants.) What we may call *failure* only occurs if we fail to learn our lessons and apply them in the future.

Struggling against karma is usually a waste of time and energy—unless you need to learn that lesson! We need to accept that even though we control much of our destiny by the choices and changes we make, sometimes Essence has other plans for us. "God asks no man whether he will accept life. This is not the choice. You must take it. The only question is how," said Henry Ward Beecher. With a focus on process as well as results, with a desire not just to achieve but to learn and grow regardless of our circumstances, we will flow through life rather than struggle. We will accept our circumstances as part of Essence's universal plan.

In the five stages of grief as described by Elisabeth Kübler-Ross, acceptance is the final step and the most important for us to reach. There's a story of a young man who was going blind. He had reached the point where doctors could do nothing more for him. A very wise doctor said with compassion, "You must learn to love your blindness." The young man's first reaction was anger and scorn. How could he love the loss of his sight? Over the next several months, he felt himself shriveling inside. Then one day, he decided to become resigned to his blindness—and something relaxed in his heart. In that space, he was able to move, step by step, from resignation to tolerance to acceptance. Finally, he was able to say to himself once again, "Blind as you are, I love you." On that day, his whole life changed.

Psychologist Carl Rogers remarked, "The curious paradox is that when I accept myself just as I am, then I can change." If we change because we hate ourselves, we are like someone who flees from an enemy on a battlefield, moving in panic in no particular direction, just as likely to end up in a worse place as we are to find safety. True change must begin with an acceptance of where we are and, more important, *who* we are. Acceptance creates a space inside, a freedom to choose the kind of change that will uplift and improve our lives. Accept yourself at the deepest level as a manifestation of Essence. See yourself as part of its perfection no matter where you are in your path toward enlightenment. Like the blind man, say to yourself, "Just as you are, I love you." And let that love lead you to seek to grow in Essence every day of your life.

What Never Changes

All things change, nothing is extinguished.

—OVID

In the *Tao Te Ching,* the great philosopher Lao-Tzu described Essence, which he called the *Tao,* as follows: "Something chaotic yet complete, which existed before Heaven and Earth. Oh, how still it is, and formless, standing alone without changing, reaching everywhere without suffering harm! It must be regarded as the Mother of the Universe." At the center of all lies Essence, the mother of the universe, that which never changes yet encompasses all change within itself. When we connect with this unchanging Essence, which is part of us and in which we exist, it can be easier to view change as a part of life. By remembering always that our essential nature is eternal and changeless, we look at even the greatest change as simply a new step in the dance that extends throughout our lifetime and beyond. We can understand more easily how the circumstances of our lives serve as the means for our growth. We can become more open to change and yet stronger and more able to withstand the highs and lows that change inevitably brings. When we connect with the unchanging space within ourselves, we're able to deal with whatever life throws at us.

Recognizing and connecting with the unchanging in the midst of change can help us in the most difficult circumstances. All of us are faced with loss and the pain of change at some point. We lose our home. The relationship we thought would last a lifetime ends. We, or someone we love, are diagnosed with a serious illness. If amid the raw emotion and pain we feel, we still can find that place within ourselves where unchanging love and goodness exists, or if we can connect with universal goodness through prayer or meditation, the edge of our pain is blunted and we can find a calm that will help us cope. When we are children and we get hurt, our natural instinct is to run to our mother or some caring adult. We know they will hold us, comfort us, and calm us. Simply being with them, we feel better because we are surrounded by their love. Essence wishes to do the same for us when we are faced with great pain. It will comfort us and hold us gently in its love, making difficult situations easier to bear.

Nowhere is it more important to focus on the unchanging love of Essence than when our dear ones pass to the other side. In those moments of great change, it can be hard to believe that our nature is imperishable and our souls eternal. We focus on what is lost because it is so present in our minds and hearts. Yet these moments can make us most aware of the eternal love that we share with our loved ones, the unchanging love that can uphold us in our grief.

There is a story of a woman who came to a Taoist master following the death of her only son. The master listened as she sobbed and spoke of her inconsolable grief. Then he took her hand. "My dear one, I cannot wipe away your tears," he said gently. "All I can do is to teach you how to make them holy." We make the changes of our lives holy by using them to connect even more deeply with Essence and can find consolation in the calm, gentle, compassionate love that envelops and uplifts both us and our loved ones on the other side.

As a last resort, if our pain is too great to understand or to bear, we can offer it up. Sometimes the only way to ease our suffering is to say to Essence, "I can't, so you must." In its eternal and unchanging love, we can experience hope, acceptance, and perhaps an understanding that there is a reason and purpose even to things we don't understand. In Psalm 130, King David wrote, "Out of the depths have I cried unto thee, O Lord. . . . My soul waiteth for the Lord more than they that watch for the morning. . . . With the Lord there is mercy, and with him is plenteous redemption." Pain points us toward the source of all consolation. Change reminds us of our unchangeable nature. If we are wise, we will regard change as the bends in the road that lead us gently yet inexorably toward our true nature and our last, best home—in the heart of Essence itself.

YOUR SOUL'S ENERGY BOOSTERS

- Change presents us with both opportunities and challenges.
- Change is a requirement of growth.
- The one thing you can count on in life is change. It is inevitable!

- Every change has the potential to create ripples far beyond ourselves and this lifetime.
- Whenever we are faced with change, Essence will support us each step of the way. Including through fear and inertia.
- Some change we may be unhappy with at first can ultimately be a blessing in disguise.
- With Essence's support and guidance, it is possible to find the blessings in our challenges.
- Our intuition can tell us if a particular change is healthy and good for us.
- Sleep on your choice if at all possible.
- Memorize the four C's: Courage, Confidence, Commitment, Conquer.
- Sometimes the biggest lessons of unexpected challenges are trust and faith.
- Even though we control most of our destiny there are some things in life that change that we must learn to accept. Most important, when we accept ourselves and who we are, true change and growth can occur.
- When a dear one passes away, remember the eternal love you had with that person. Offer your suffering to Essence and find consolation in the calm, gentle, compassionate love that envelops and uplifts us and our loved ones on the other side.

TEN

The Heart of Essence: Gratitude and Giving

If the only prayer you say in your whole life is "Thank you," that would suffice.

—MEISTER ECKHART

Have you ever walked into a magnificent cathedral, mosque, synagogue, or temple and felt God's presence? Have you ever held your child in your arms, or looked into the eyes of the love of your life? Have you stood at the top of a mountain or on the seashore and watched in awe as the sun rose into the heavens and the world seemed to begin anew? Have you witnessed the selfless devotion of caregivers who minister to people with tenderness and respect, or the bravery of firefighters, police officers, or soldiers who risk their lives to save others? Have you ever gone through a difficult time, only to look back and realize that Essence had been your unseen partner every step of the way? In those moments that we connect to love, awe, beauty, devotion, and goodness, gratitude is our natural response. When we feel grateful, we are acknowledging the gifts we have been given in our lives. Gratitude is "the homage of the heart rendered to God for his goodness," wrote American poet Nathaniel P. Willis. Gratitude humbles and touches us at our core. It puts us in tune with the vibrations of the universe. In chapter 5 I mentioned Japanese scientist and businessman Masaru Emoto. He has shown the effects of just the words *love* and *gratitude* upon water. He put purified water in glass containers upon which he had written *love* and *gratitude.* After allowing the water to sit for a few hours, he froze droplets to form ice crystals and then photographed the crystals before they melted. The crystals made from regular purified water looked pretty, but the water that had been exposed to the words *love* and *gratitude* formed crystals of enormous beauty and symmetry. "It was as if the water had rejoiced and celebrated by creating a flower in bloom," Emoto wrote.

The emotion of gratitude unites us not only with Essence but also with our loved ones here and on the other side. When we send our loving thoughts to departed friends and family, one of the sweetest and most healing things we can say is, "Thank you for being part of my life. Thank you for sharing your love. Thank you for meaning so much to me." Such sentiments can be difficult to express in the first few days of grief, but they can serve as an integral part of a memorial service or funeral. Love is a blessing, and its natural corollary is gratitude for receiving that love. From the readings I've done, it's clear that our loved ones on the other side continue to feel gratitude. I saw an example of this not too long ago. One young man, Jan, who had lost his parents at an early age, wanted to know if they watched over him and approved of his life. His mother and father came through quickly to tell him they loved him and approved his choices in a career and a partner. But then they had another message for Jan's sister, Wilhelmina, who was with him at the reading. "You took over the family when they died, didn't you?" I asked Wilhelmina. "You were like another mother to Jan, and they want you to know you've done a beautiful job. Their arms are embracing you, and they're crying because they're so grateful. They will look out for both of you, and they love you very much." The smiles on the faces of Jan and Wilhelmina told me how much it meant to them to hear their parents' message.

i thank You God for most this amazing
day: for the leaping greenly spirits of trees
and a blue true dream of sky; and for everything
which is natural which is infinite which is yes
—e. e. cummings

Gratitude enriches our lives whenever we choose to feel it. No matter how difficult our lives, they become easier and better if we can find something to be grateful for. It can start with the treasures we perhaps take for granted. How many mornings do we say, "Thank you," before we get out of bed? Most of us wake up thinking about our first cup of coffee, or everything we need to accomplish, or how long before we need to get to work rather than simply being grateful that we have been given another day of life. How many of us say "Thank you" for our bodies? Most of the time, we take our bodies for granted until we get sick, but they are a priceless gift, the vehicle in which our souls live and grow and learn. "Would you sell both your eyes for a million dollars . . . or your two legs . . . or your hands . . . or your hearing? Add up what you do have, and you'll find that you won't sell them for all the gold in the world," wrote Dale Carnegie. Even our troubles and difficulties are gifts of Essence and should be received with gratitude whenever possible. Think about the tough times in your life. When viewed from your perspective today, how many of them were filled with gifts of understanding or growth? Everything that comes into our lives can be regarded as a gift if we choose to look for the purpose of Essence that lies beneath it. And whether or not we see the immediate purpose, the act of our gratitude can make it easier to accept what comes our way. I have seen this with people who have gone through horrendous events—the loss of children, murders of loved ones, accidents that have wiped out their hopes. One of the most significant parts of the healing process occurs when we can remember the love we shared with those who are gone and think with gratitude of the gift these departed souls were in our lives. When we focus on love and gratitude instead of loss, we open ourselves to rediscover the part of our loved ones that never dies, that will always be with us, and that will be waiting for us on the other side.

Ultimately, we should feel most grateful for the gift of our awareness of the presence of Essence in our lives. In Hinduism, it's believed that we must go through millions of incarnations as plants, insects, and animals until our souls evolve enough to be born in human form. Then it takes tens of thousands of lifetimes until our souls become aware of our spiritual nature and begin the process of consciously choosing to become more like Essence. If you are reading this book, I believe that you have come a long way in your evolution as a spiritual being simply because you seek something more than just what you experience in this world. Rejoice in the gift of Essence: as Alexander MacLaren wrote, "Seek to cultivate a buoyant, joyous sense of the crowded kindnesses of God in your daily life." Be grateful for the glimpses you have of your own Essential nature. Your gratitude will make you more aware of everything you are receiving, opening you to receive and give more. Gratitude inevitably opens the door for greater gifts. It's like an upward spiral that lifts us closer to Essence both within ourselves and in our evolution from lifetime to lifetime.

Circulating the Gifts of the Universe

Life is given to us, we earn it by giving it.

—RABINDRANATH TAGORE

Love, goodness, and wisdom may be the fundamental elements of Essence, but giving is its nature. There is something in every part of the universe that is driven to give, whether it is a flower that gives its beauty, a tree that gives its shade, plants that give their nourishment, animals that look out for their young and for one another. A friend of a friend visited India for the first time recently, and at a small temple in the countryside, she saw a monkey with a bowlful of food. (Monkeys in the region are wild and very bold; they steal food from both children and adults, and no one bothers them because they bite.) This monkey held the food bowl in one hand, and in the other it held a tiny puppy. At first, the woman thought the monkey was going to hurt the puppy, but then she realized it was petting the puppy, holding the bowl so the puppy could eat from it and turning the bowl so it could reach all the food. What an amazing instance of kindness from one creature to another! It reminded this woman that giving seems to be part of every species and every form of life. By living in an attitude of gratitude, we are aligning ourselves with this energy of Essence. It's as if we are closing a circuit between Essence and ourselves, making a perfect connection that elevates us and brings us closer to who we really are.

Since our task on Earth is to continually progress in our likeness to Essence, to learn and grow in goodness, love, and wisdom, and since Essence's fundamental nature is to give, it must be ours as well. Gratitude should be accompanied by responsibility; we must both be thankful and in turn share our bounty with others as Essence has shared its bounty with us. It's no accident that spiritual writings from every tradition emphasize the requirement to give to others. It's considered one of the pillars of Islam to give *zakat,* or "poor tax," a small percentage of the value of income and assets, every year. In the Koran, a righteous man is defined as "he who believes in God and the Last Day, in the angels and the Book and the prophets; who, though he loves it dearly, gives away his wealth to kinsfolk, to orphans, to the destitute, to the traveler in need and to beggars, and for the redemption of captives; who attends to his prayers and renders the alms levy" (The Cow, 2:177).

I grew up in a Jewish family, where I learned about the idea of tzedakah. The word literally means *righteousness,* but nowadays it's used to denote charity or tithing, giving a certain percentage of your yearly income to those in need. Leviticus, Numbers, and Deuteronomy are three of the great law-giving books of the Torah, and they require that Jews give to the needy. At every harvest, Jews were bidden to go through their fields and vines only once and leave the gleanings for the "stranger, the fatherless, and the widow." Tzedakah is a religious obligation that must be performed by all, even the poorest. It's a way of gaining the favor of the Almighty and a cornerstone of spiritual life. "Give generously to [your brother] and do so without a grudging heart; because of this the Lord your God will bless you in all your work and in everything you put your hand to" (Deuteronomy 15:10).

In many traditions, giving to others is equal in importance, if not more important, than giving to God. After all, God doesn't need what we have to give; it's all God's already! But when we help others in their time of need, we become the hands of God, which is what God wishes. In the New Testament, Jesus described the welcome waiting the generous and righteous in heaven because "I was hungry, and ye gave me meat: I was thirsty and ye gave me drink: I was a stranger, and ye took me in: Naked, and ye clothed me: I was sick, and ye visited me: I was in prison, and ye came unto me." And when the righteous asked God when they had done these things, God replies, "Inasmuch as ye have done it unto one of the least of these my brethren, ye have done it unto me" (Matthew 25:34–40).

There's a story of a great Buddhist master, Tetsugen, who wanted to translate into Japanese and publish several holy books that were available only in Chinese. The project would take a great deal of money, so Tetsugen went from town to town to collect donations. After ten years, he had amassed enough funds, and the work of translation began. Just then, the main river in the province flooded and destroyed most of the crops. There was no food, and people were starving. Tetsugen took the money he had collected, used it to buy rice, and distributed it to the hungry. Then he left home once more to gather funds so the translation could proceed.

After a few years more, he had almost enough money to return home when an epidemic hit. Thousands of children were left without support. Once again, Tetsugen used the money for the translation to help families who were in need. Then for a third time, he left home to collect money for translating and publishing the sacred books. After almost thirty years, the project was completed. Tetsugen died shortly afterward, a happy man. However, there are those who say that the lives he helped with the money for the first two "editions" were even more sacred than the books themselves.

Just as it is easy to get caught up in the day-to-day routines of life and forget to be grateful for all we are given, we also can forget how much we have and how much of a difference even a small contribution can make. We're so focused on what we want and what we think we need that we make giving our last priority rather than our first. But giving to others first should be just as important as taking care of our own needs. How many of us make our daily latte more of a priority than charity? Even the smallest amount can make a difference to someone. And if we can't donate money, what else can we give? There's an Arab proverb that says, "If you have much, give of your wealth; if you have little, give of your heart." How many occasions has your life been brightened by a kind word or smile that cost nothing yet meant so much? The gift of our time and attention can be even more important than the gift of our funds, and certainly it is more personal. How much would it mean to someone who has a family member in the hospital or who has just lost a loved one if you were to deliver a homemade casserole, or volunteer to run errands, or pick someone up from the airport, or take the children to the zoo for an afternoon, or visit the hospital and sit with the one who is ill so that others can take a break? I know of many Jewish nurses and doctors who volunteer to work Christmas Day so their Christian colleagues can be home with their families. And if you've ever volunteered to serve meals in a homeless shelter on a holiday, you can see how much it means to these souls that someone cares enough to give their time to those less fortunate. "Give what you have," poet Henry Wadsworth Longfellow directs us. "To someone, it may be better than you dare to think."

A few months ago, I was at home in Michigan. It was cold and snowy, and I was walking down one of the streets of the town where I live. I saw a homeless man standing next to a building. In front of him was a small, hand-lettered sign that read, "HUNGRY: PLEASE HELP." I didn't have a lot of cash with me, but I had just been to the grocery story and had a loaf of bread in my car. I went to the car, took out the bread, and hurried back to the homeless man. When I gave it to him, you would have thought I had just given him a million dollars, he was so grateful. But he wasn't happy simply because he now had something to eat; he was happy that someone had seen him and cared about his situation.

Shakespeare once wrote about mercy, "It is twice blessed: / It blesseth him that gives and him that takes." The same may be said when we are kind to others. Acts of kindness make us feel good. Usually, there is no reciprocity involved in an act of kindness; we simply do something for another for no benefit to ourselves. What we do receive, however, is the happiness that comes when we are kind. Kindness is goodness and love in action. We can be kind to anyone—the homeless person on the street, the people we love more than anyone else on earth, strangers and relatives, animals, the environment, and so on. When we focus on being kind, we'll discover that the universe will present us with dozens of opportunities to make a difference in small ways. "The best portion of a good man's life are / His little, nameless, unremembered acts / Of kindness and of love," wrote William Wordsworth. We get closest to Essence through our random acts of anonymous kindness. The littlest things, like taking ten minutes of your busy day to chat with the lonely old lady next door, or making time in your day to help someone in need, can make a difference for someone else and elevate our souls closer to the angels.

> He who receives a benefit with gratitude repays
> the first installment on his debt.
>
> —SENECA

To be in tune with Essence, we need to be good receivers as well as good givers. This can be difficult. Giving almost always makes us feel good, but it can be hard at times to receive, even if we are in need. Feeling that we are in someone's debt with little or no chance to repay them can be hard on the ego. Tony Robbins tells a story of when he was nine years old and his family was going through a very difficult period. It was Thanksgiving, his dad was out of work, and there was no food in the house. In the middle of the day, Tony heard a knock at the door. When he opened it, he saw a man standing on the porch with a big box of food. "I'm from the church down the way, and we heard your family was having a tough time. This is for your Thanksgiving," the man said.

"Just a minute!" Tony replied, and ran to get his dad, excitedly pulling him to the door to see the unexpected bounty. But as soon as his father saw the man with the box, his face darkened. "We don't accept charity!" he snapped, and slammed the door shut. That event made an indelible mark on the young Tony. He was so grateful for the stranger who had wanted to help his family that he vowed to do the same anonymously and deliver food in such a way that the receiver could keep their pride. For the past thirty years, he personally has delivered food to families in need and the homeless at Thanksgiving. His foundation sponsors "Basket Brigades" all over the world, where groups of people get together to prepare food baskets to distribute on holidays. Every basket is delivered anonymously; with the givers acting as delivery people with no knowledge of where the food came from. Inside each basket is a note that reads, "This was prepared by someone who loves you. We ask only that one day you do the same for someone else."

In truth, everything in our lives is a gift, the result of someone else's efforts on our behalf. We are given love by our families and friends. Someone's labor created the houses we live in and the cars we drive, the clothes we wear and the possessions we enjoy. We have electricity because someone makes sure the turbines run and generators operate smoothly. We have food because of the labors of farmers, growers, shippers, and merchants. All things exist because of the gifts of sun and light and rain and nature. "Many times a day I realize how much my own life is built on the labors of my fellowmen, and how earnestly I must exert myself in order to give in return as much as I have received," wrote Albert Einstein. We must receive the gifts of the universe with gratitude and make sure we are a part of the never-ending cycle of giving and receiving. This includes protecting our planet from climate change and global warming.

When we truly understand giving and receiving, we recognize the truth that lies behind the Golden Rule: there is no difference between us and our neighbors. When we feel the oneness of the human race, we develop compassion and a sense of connection with everyone and everything. We see giving and receiving as a great cycle essential for growth. Essence wants us to be both cheerful givers and cheerful receivers, and to experience and express gratitude in both circumstances. "To help all created things, that is the measure of our responsibility; to be helped by all, that is the measure of our hope," wrote Father Gerald Vann. Living the Golden Rule and understanding the true relationship between giving, receiving, and gratitude will help us live, grow, and learn in the way Essence intended, as part of the great circle of life, energy, and love.

Why—and How—Are You Giving?

The manner of giving is worth more than the gift.

—PIERRE CORNEILLE

It's pretty clear that Essence wants us to give and receive—but what do we choose to give, and how do we choose to give it? Equally important, how should we receive? I believe there are different traits of Essence-based giving and receiving. First, *it must draw us closer to Essence rather than feeding the ego.* I'm sure you've seen people who give only when they are acknowledged for it. They get a rush from seeing their name on the side of a building or at the top of a donation list, or they make a big deal every time they do something for someone else. Even though they protest and say, "It's nothing—don't mention it!" they make sure you know it's a big deal to them. Even the smallest favor or gift becomes a way of stroking their egos. Such favors tend to create resentment rather than gratitude; they make us feel small because the givers need to feel so big. However, giving should not be a competitive sport or a means of ego gratification. Many great souls give anonymously, and no one ever knows about their generosity until after they are gone. There was a gentleman who lived in the middle of the United States. Every Christmas, he would put on a Santa suit, hat, and beard, and walk along the snowy streets of his city and give away fifty-dollar bills. He gave away millions of dollars in this manner, anonymously. No one ever knew who he was until after he passed away. Today, a friend of his continues his tradition of anonymous giving. In the New Testament, Jesus tells us that when we give, our left hand should not know what our right hand is doing. If we give in secret, he says, God will see and reward us openly (Matthew 6:3–4). I believe that when we give unselfishly, we are acting as Essence's agent; we become a conduit of abundance from the universe. Do we feel good when we give? Of course—and that is our reward. But our good feelings should have very little to do with how much we are acknowledged and far more to do with the fact that giving connects us with our true nature. We should feel grateful for having been given the opportunity to partner with Essence in spreading its bounty to others. When we give, we should simply enjoy the beauty of the giving or helping or healing or caring, and set aside anything that separates us from that pure experience of Essence.

> Giving to others selflessly and anonymously, radiating light throughout the world and illuminating your own darkness, your virtue becomes a sanctuary for yourself and all beings.
>
> —LAO-TZU

Second, *Essence-based giving is selfless.* I remember seeing a documentary about a famine in Africa that showed a small boy who had fought his way to the front of a food line to get a bowl of some kind of stew. He went around the corner and brought the bowl to his younger brother, letting his brother eat before he himself had any morsel of what he had worked so hard to get. In *Man's Search for Meaning,* psychologist Viktor Frankl described the horrors of living in a concentration camp in World War II—but he also told of prisoners who gave away their own bread ration to those who were worse off. Selfless actions like these trigger our awareness of the godliness and goodness that humanity is capable of, if we only act upon our highest instincts. Such acts of invisible giving happen every day. Think of family members who care for someone with Alzheimer's or diseases like multiple sclerosis. Think of parents of children with genetic illnesses or birth defects, and the loving care they offer these innocents day after day, year after year. In situations such as these, giving could give rise to resentment or anger or complaining about fate. But when we give selflessly, such feelings, while natural, are usually temporary. Our circumstances can become the means to connect with the support of Essence, which will sustain us through our trials. If we give expecting nothing in return, we will receive everything.

> I don't know what your destiny will be but one thing I do know: The only ones among you who will be happy are those who have sought and found how to serve.
>
> —ALBERT SCHWEITZER

Third, *service to others is a high form of giving.* As part of Essence, we are called to serve others and help them to learn, grow, and discover the truth of who they are. Service puts our gratitude into concrete form. "Your work is love made visible," wrote Kahlil Gibran. Service offered freely is literally love in action. But just like giving of our time and money or anything else, our service must be offered without expectation of return. Lao-Tzu said that service to others without expectation of reward is one of the four cardinal virtues of life. "To practice virtue is to selflessly offer assistance to others, giving without limitation one's time, abilities, and possessions in service, whenever and wherever needed, without prejudice concerning the identity of those in need," he wrote. In the Indian religious tradition, this kind of service is called *seva,* or action offered to the divine selflessly, with no strings. When you do something as an offering, work becomes a sacred act. Whether you're scrubbing floors, taking care of children or the sick, or doing business, you perform your task to the best of your ability without expectation of acknowledgment or reward, because it's your gift to the divine. You also do it without attachment to the results: you do your best and leave the rest up to God. Work becomes a means of connecting you to Essence, and every action becomes an opportunity for joy.

> The greatest good you can do for another is not just to share your riches, but to reveal to him his own.
>
> —BENJAMIN DISRAELI

Fourth, *Essence-based giving helps people become more.* We've all heard the old proverb, "Give a man a fish and he eats for a day; teach him to fish and he eats for a lifetime." How will your gift help this person grow? Does your gift support them in continuing bad habits or fostering dependency, or does it put them on the path of self-sufficiency? A gift designed to help people raise themselves up says, "I believe in you. I regard you as my equal. I'm simply here to be the stepping-stone that gets you back on your feet." This kind of giving honors the receiver as well as the giver. It creates a relationship of equality, of commonality, of clear energy between two people. In this space, it's far easier for both giver and receiver to see the gift for what it is: Essence sharing itself with Essence.

Fifth, *Essence-based giving is done with joy.* "The Lord loves a cheerful giver," proclaimed Paul in 2 Corinthians. If you've given something grudgingly, you know there is no pleasure in the giving, nor does the receiver take it with pleasure. It's better to give less and give with love than it is to give more unwillingly. "It's not how much we give but how much love we put into giving," Mother Teresa said. Remember, Essence gives freely to us all, sharing abundance from its inexhaustible supply. When we give with joy, we link ourselves to the wellspring of love and abundance that lies at our heart and fuels the universe. We connect both with humanity and the divine in one beautiful moment.

What Is Your Purpose?

The place God calls you to is the place where your deep gladness and the world's deep hunger meet.

—FREDERICK BUECHNER

The ultimate gift we give to Essence is ourselves—how we grow and what we accomplish on Earth. Someone once said that every life is either an example or a warning, and it's our responsibility to make sure that we fall into the first category rather than the second. To do so, we must do our best to live in alignment with Essence and exemplify its characteristics. We must be role models who embody goodness, wisdom, and love. We must find and fulfill the purpose for which we were born. Our purpose depends on our karma and what we chose to do before we came to Earth this time around. Our purpose doesn't have to be grand, though it certainly can be. One person's purpose may be to save a kitten from starving on the street, while another's purpose could be to save the tigers from extinction. Your purpose could be to be a great parent, or to take care of your aged parents, or to inspire others, or to build cities, or to serve the homeless, or any of a hundred thousand other paths. The key to our purpose is threefold. The primary purpose of every life is to learn and grow closer to Essence. Our secondary purpose is to work through the karma we brought with us, and to act in ways that will create good karma for our next lifetime. And our third purpose is to help others to learn and grow in Essence as well.

Living our threefold purpose is not easy. Life is a school, and we're here to learn, and our lessons can get harder, not easier, as we progress on the path to reunion with Essence. But it's only as we face and overcome greater and greater challenges that we can learn how great we truly are. "God brings men into deep waters not to drown them, but to cleanse them," wrote clergyman James H. Aughey. The universe knows what we need to learn—we can only hope to handle our trials and tribulations in such a way as to be a proud example of Essence in the world. We must learn to direct our thoughts, our emotions, and our actions so they continually lead both us and others to a greater identification with Essence.

Living to the Fullest

Don't count the days—make the days count.

—MUHAMMAD ALI

Even though we know that this lifetime is finite, most of us walk around as if we had all the time in the world to live, love, act, and give. But often we are reminded otherwise by events that tear at our hearts—like Marianne, a woman in her thirties who found her husband lying dead in their bed. He had been healthy and happy, but he passed away from an undiagnosed physical ailment. Marianne was devastated for two reasons. First, she did not believe in any kind of afterlife and so thought her husband was gone forever. Second, she worried about her two young sons who would miss their father's love. She came to me for a reading, and within a minute or two, her husband came through me to allay both fears.

"Your husband's telling me that he hugs his boys every night," I said. "Ask your son if that's not true."

The boy nodded. "I feel Dad hug me," he said. "And I made a candle for my dad and when it burned, it melted into the shape of a heart. That was my dad telling me that he loved me."

"Your husband wants so much for you to know that he loves you, and he's with you always," I told Marianne.

"Knowing that, and looking at my boys, I know that life is worth living," she replied.

The great reality I deal with every day and that most of us forget is that even though our spirit and soul never die, we are here for a limited time and death is inevitable. Our actions may shorten or lengthen our days, but death will come. While life is finite, Essence is eternal, and there is part of us that exists eternally. The form will change while spirit will remain, passing through the great change of death and moving whole and complete to the other side. That being true, the wise have no fear of death. As a great master asked on his deathbed, "Why should I keep a candle lit when the day itself is dawning?" Though we cannot see the day of the other side, we can feel its light inside ourselves, in the presence of Essence. And if we nurture our connection with Essence, when it comes time to merge our light with its light, we will have little to fear.

Use the light to return to the Light.
Then you can die yet be ever living.

—ANONYMOUS

Our primary task on Earth is to live to the fullest—meaning that we strive to become more like Essence every day. Essence is like the seed inside us, the perennial seed that grows, blooms, withers, and dies, only to grow again. A tulip bulb lies dormant in the earth over the winter, then grows and blooms in spring. Once its flower is gone, the leaves thrive until fall, when they, too, die. In winter, it looks as if the tulip is dead, but come spring it will bloom again. The Essence of the tulip is unchanging no matter what form it currently holds. Our Essence likewise is unchanging no matter what our form in this lifetime. But unlike the tulip, we can become clearer, stronger, more like Essence in goodness, wisdom, and love.

When we live to the fullest, we purify our nature by getting rid of anything that does not exist in harmony with Essence. Like a gardener who cuts back a tree or plant so that the remaining stock is stronger, we, too, must look at life as our opportunity to nurture those parts of ourselves that are like Essence and cut away anything that does not support the highest and best. That is our task, and that is our destiny. Free will can take us away from Essence and move us toward evil, but for that to happen, we must continually make bad choices lifetime after lifetime. And always Essence beckons us, asking us to become like itself. Choosing Essence is not always the easiest path, but it is the natural one. And when we choose the way of Essence, we are fulfilling the destiny for which we were born.

For all that has been, Thanks.
For all that shall be, Yes.
—DAG HAMMARSKJÖLD

Gratitude, giving and receiving, and finding and living your purpose are all aspects of a life fully lived. Essence doesn't want us to renounce life, live in a cave, meditate twenty-four hours a day, and focus only on our inner spiritual life. We are born into this world to be with others, to learn from others, to teach others, and to learn from this miraculous privilege of human birth. "Just to be is a blessing. Just to live is holy," wrote Abraham Heschel. Every day contains blessings, opportunities to grow, moments of enlightenment that show us our true nature. With a little attention, a little work, and a lot of gratitude and love, we can turn even the most commonplace day into a miracle. We can recognize and celebrate the gift of life that we have been given. Living fully isn't just for ourselves, however; it's also for the good we can do in the world. U.S. president Woodrow Wilson said, "You are not here to merely make a living. You are here in order to enable the world to live more amply, with greater vision, with a finer spirit of hope and achievement. You are here to enrich the world, and you impoverish yourself if you forget the errand." Every day, we make a choice about the way we will live and how we will impact the world and those around us. Will we take the time to offer even the smallest assistance to another? Will we choose to act from love or from hate? Will we make others' needs at least equal to our own, if not more important? I'm not saying that we must always live completely for others; we have to recognize and acknowledge our own value as well as the value of the beings that share our path. However, Essence wants us to be a living example of love in action. It wants us to be, do, and live as our best so we can help and inspire those around us. Essence wants us to reach, strive, grow, become, and make a difference.

And Essence won't allow us to wait. The clock is ticking; we have only a certain amount of life given to us. How we use it will determine the progress we make this time around, so choose to do good now. A beautiful young girl once wrote, "How wonderful it is that nobody need wait a single moment before starting to improve the world!" Her name was Anne Frank, and the gift of her story and spirit are continuing to inspire millions. What are you choosing to do with the years you have been given? I once heard someone say that our job on Earth is simple: live, love, laugh, and leave a lasting legacy. Essence wants us to rejoice, to dance, to be uplifted as we uplift others. Living in wisdom and light daily should make us happy, because it reassures us that we are something more than what we see, that our spirits expand out from our small, localized, locked-in-time awareness into the field of infinite possibilities and all-compassionate love. That is who we are, and all we need to do is to open our awareness to its presence and then act in accordance with its heart.

One of my favorite movies is *The Wizard of Oz*—I love the songs, the story, and the message. In it, Dorothy is plucked from her home in Kansas and whirled through the air into a strange yet beautiful land. She must make her way through great dangers and adventures to the Emerald City. Along the road, she meets comrades who help her and whom she helps in turn. But every step of the way, her goal is to return home where she belongs. Dorothy is given the task of killing the Wicked Witch of the West. Even though she faces great danger in her quest, she kills the witch and frees all the people who have suffered under the witch's rule. Finally, she returns to the Emerald City and claims her reward of being able to go home. But at that moment, Glinda, the good witch, tells Dorothy, "You've always had the power to go back to Kansas." To the Scarecrow, she adds, "She had to learn it for herself."

Dorothy's journey is our journey. We, too, leave our eternal home and take birth in this strange and wonderful world. We must make our way through dangers and adventures, through beautiful fields and dark forests. We will meet true comrades and some enemies along the way, and we will help and be helped by those we meet. Our ultimate goal is always to get back home, but we must learn our lessons first. When we do, we will discover that we had the power to return home all along. The part of eternity that we carry with us inside, that bit of Essence, is like the ruby slippers that we wear without recognizing their power. But when we acknowledge our Essence and attune ourselves to its goodness, wisdom, and love, it will always lead us "over the rainbow" and back to our eternal home.

YOUR SOUL'S ENERGY BOOSTERS

- The emotion of gratitude unites us not only with Essence but also with our loved ones here and on the other side.
- Gratitude enriches our lives whenever we choose to feel it.
- We should feel most grateful for the gift of our awareness of the presence of Essence in our inner lives.
- Your gratitude will make you more aware of everything you are receiving and inevitably open the door for greater gifts.

- Love, goodness and wisdom may be the fundamental elements of Essence, but giving is its nature.
- By living in an attitude of gratitude, we are aligning ourselves with this energy of Essence.
- When we help others in time of need, we become the hands of God, which is what God wishes.
- Everything in our lives is a gift, the result of someone else's efforts on our behalf.
- Giving to others selflessly and anonymously, radiating light throughout the world and illuminating your own darkness, your virtue becomes a sanctuary for yourself and all beings.
- Essence-based giving is selfless.
- Service to others is a high form of giving.
- Essence-based giving helps people grow.
- We must also learn to receive gifts with gratitude. Giving and receiving are essential for growth.
- Essence-based giving is done with joy.
- We must find and fulfill the purpose for which we were born. Our purpose depends on our karma and what we chose to do before we came to Earth this time around.
- Life is a school and we are here to learn, and our lessons get harder, not easier, as we progress on the path to reunion with Essence.
- When we live to the fullest, we purify our nature by getting rid of anything that does not exist in harmony with Essence.

- Gratitude, giving and receiving, and finding your purpose are all aspects of a life fully lived.
- Every day we make a choice about the way we will live and how we will impact the world and those around us.

ACKNOWLEDGMENTS

Over my forty-five-plus years of work as a spiritual intuitive, there have been many great souls who have contributed to the journey. A big thanks to my incredible editor, Joel Fotinos, and his assistant, Gwen Hawkes. A special thanks to Jennifer Enderlin for her continued support of my work and a huge thanks to the entire St. Martin's Press family. It takes a village. Thanks go to my trusted writing partner, Victoria St. George of Just Write, who always seems to know exactly what to say in the way I want to say it. Thanks to my trusted attorney, Chase Mellen III, and my manager, Gina Rugolo.

In my office in Michigan, thanks to Nicole Smith, my assistant, whose priceless loyalty and relentless hard work allows me to help other people. Also to John Edward, for his insight and assistance in my search for her.

Friends and family are the most important parts of my life, so unending thanks to my sisters, Alicia Tisdale (who helped with final edits) and Elaine Lippitt, for keeping the goodness and purity of our parents' Essence alive, as well as their families and all my amazing friends. Including Chris Colfer, who I adore, and who thanked ME in HIS best-selling book! Stuart Krasnow, for his loving friendship and continued support of my work. To Tony Sweet, for helping to make CharVision a success. Special thanks to Tom Campbell and World of Wonder for producing *Reading Queens with Char Margolis*. My deepest gratitude to RuPaul, for writing a heartwarming foreword, and to Michael Patrick King, for his supportive friendship. I can't forget my psychic sidekick, my chihuahua mix, Sunny Margolis, who shows me unconditional love every day.

As always, my deepest thanks go to the thousands of people who have opened their lives and hearts and given me the privilege of reading for them. With each reading, we have the opportunity together to touch Essence both here and on the other side. Their stories are an integral part of this book, and I hope they will inspire readers one-tenth as much as they have touched and inspired me. Their examples remind us of the goodness, wisdom, and love that connect us all.

For inquiries about private readings, group sessions, or speaking events, contact Char at www.Char.net

Follow Char on:

www.Facebook.com/IntuitiveMediumCharMargolis

Twitter: @PsychicMedmChar

www.Instagram.com/CharMargolis

www.Youtube.com/c/CharMargolisPsychicIntuitiveMedium

ABOUT THE AUTHOR

Paul Smith

Char Margolis is an internationally acclaimed Intuitive-Medium who has been stunning audiences for decades with her gift to connect to the spirit world. Char currently stars on *Reading Queens with Char Margolis* on Wow Presents Plus and also has a weekly radio/web show *CharVision,* which explores all things metaphysical, spiritual, and paranormal. She has been on numerous talk shows, including *Dr. Phil, Dr. Oz*, and the *Today* show.

Victoria St. George of Just Write is a writer and editor living in San Diego, California.